# ICI Dulux

# COLOUR

## WITH CONFIDENCE

This edition published exclusively for
Imperial Chemical Industries plc by
Orbis Book Publishing Corporation Limited,
a member of BPCC plc.

Designed by Judith Highton
Illustrations by Hayward Art Group
Text by Linda Gray, Judy Martin,
Mary Trewby and Celia Rufey
Editorial management by Renny Harrop
Edited by Jenny Jones

Text © 1987 Orbis Book Publishing
Corporation Limited
Photographic © 1987 Imperial Chemical
Industries plc
Paints Division, Wexham Road,
Slough, SL2 5DS
© ICI/Dulux is a trademark of ICI plc
Colour reproduction by Colorlito, Milan
Printed in Great Britain

ISBN 0356 147 746

# INTRODUCTION

Say the word 'paint', and automatically you think of Dulux. That's because Dulux have always produced paint that's a byword for quality and an ever-increasing colour range. Now, with the help of this book, they want to take you one step further into the world of colour, to help you realize its full potential and enable you to make the most of colour in your home.

Over the years, Dulux found that many of their customers were more concerned about the effects of the paint colour they had chosen than how to apply it or choose a particular finish. As a result, the Company introduced three special products to help you choose the right colours for your home. Colour Testers are mini pots of paint with built-in brushes that are the ideal samplers to use at home, so you can see exactly how the colour in a paint chart looks on your walls. The *Come Home To Colour* pack not only includes useful practical advice but also extra-large edge-matched chips to help you plan your colour scheme, and the *At Home With Colour* video gives you a unique visual guide to using colours to their best advantage.

Now, Dulux have produced this book, *Colour with Confidence,* which contains everything you need to know about colour in the home. It begins by illustrating the different families of colour, so you can see how hues relate to each other and discover the ways in which they affect your moods. When you've decided which you prefer and which you'd rather avoid, turn to the next section, which shows you how to create colour schemes and gives you some invaluable interior design

The light and warmth of these subtle, harmonious colours contribute to the atmosphere of this welcoming hall.

tricks of the trade. Move on to the room-to-room guide to see decorating schemes in action – whether your home is big or small, formal or cosy, you'll find plenty of inspiration. With the accent on practicality, there's advice on dealing with rooms of different shapes and sizes as well as ideas on planning rooms and devising lighting systems. Finally, study the practical chapter which tells you how to decorate both the inside and outside of your home, so you can take real pride in the scheme you've chosen so carefully. There's plenty of information for the novice as well as the experienced decorator, plus a simple, step-by-step guide to all the newest paint treatments, from sponging and ragging to colour washing, to help you introduce pattern to the world of paint.

*Colour with Confidence* has been planned to help everyone with an interest in design, whether you're starting from scratch and need a comprehensive guide to using colour at home, want visual inspiration to spark off your imagination or are looking for clear, concise and practical advice. You don't need special training or a flair for colour to create schemes that please you and your family – just let this book bring out your natural talent and taste. You'll quickly discover as you read through it that your choice of colour can work for you in many ways. It can add warmth and atmosphere to a room, create a sense of drama or a feeling of peace, increase its light, disguise problem areas or even bring down the ceiling! Colour is the greatest ally you can have in home decorating – all you need is a pot of paint.

Happy decorating!

# CLOSE-UP ON

COLOUR

What's your favourite colour? The first that springs to mind is probably one of the colours of the rainbow – red, orange, yellow, green, blue or violet – but these represent just a few of the thousands of shades from which you can choose. Colour has always been recognized as one of the most important elements in decoration, but we are the first generation to be able to exploit its full potential. Though we were painting walls before we climbed out of the caves, it's only in the past 30 years that we have been able to buy paint, furnishings and fabrics in the entire spectrum of colours. There are now 500 paint shades available for DIY use alone – compare this palette with the restricted range of colours used by early decorators who had to be content with shades produced by natural dyes. It's common to visualize period decor in pastel tones but this is far from the truth. In fact houses were often decorated in vivid colours but they faded or yellowed fast. Country cottages were distempered in red and yellow ochre which soon softened to pink and buttermilk, while even the classical statues and temples we think of as white were once brightly painted. When paint was first produced commercially the favourite shades were buff, sky blue, green and brown – a typical colour scheme for a Georgian house was an unlikely combination of chocolate and green!

Synthetic dyes increased the range but they were often bright and crude. One of these, magenta, was aptly named after a battle in 1859 – they must have known it would fight with other colours!

Two rooms which sing with colour. Peach and blue create an inviting mood, left, while the colours are intensified for drama, above.

Dark shades were dominant for practical reasons to conceal the dirt; only the rich could afford to use pastels. Not that many were available; brilliant white paint was not produced until the Twenties when all-white rooms became the ultimate in chic. Though boarding-house brown was the norm, the potential of colour was demonstrated by the pacesetters.

As home ownership increased, the boom in home improvement began. Not only did it add value to homes, but housebuyers discovered the satisfaction of creating an environment that reflected their own taste rather than the landlady's. Britain became a nation addicted to DIY (it's still top of the league today), happy to change from Festival of Britain – style black, yellow and red to pale blue and primrose in the Fifties, orange and purple in the Sixties and brown and beige in the Seventies. Although from the early Eighties onwards grey has become the fashionable neutral while the new natural whites provide an alternative to the brilliant white which has always been top favourite, now all the signs are that we're becoming bolder and want to add more colour to our homes.

But which colour? The choice has never been greater. There are the natural whites; or look at pink, from rose to deep cranberry. Consider apricot and peach; green ranging from celadon to vivid lime; or blue, from sky blue to dark navy. Greys and browns come in many shades too, and, finally, there are the dramatic purples and reds. Let's look at these colours individually to assess their impact, and your reaction to them. Turn the page to see which best suits you, and your family home.

Softer than white, paler than pastels – the natural whites contain just a hint of colour to make the most of light and space. Above all, they're easy to live with, and make ideal partners for any colour scheme. The easiest way to use them is to create a room based around one colour, blending a range of tones so that they merge into each other. Nothing could be prettier than a bedroom decorated in palest pink – or blue, or yellow – with paintwork, walls, carpet, curtains and bedlinen to match. Deepen the colours for practicality downstairs, teaming pale walls and woodwork with a darker carpet and adding pattern for interest in living room curtains and upholstery. Keep to shades of the same colour and the scheme will be a sure success; match rose-white walls with a raspberry carpet – or vice versa – and add lace, chintz or candy-striped curtains.

If you want to contrast rather than co-ordinate, try the natural whites for the subtlest of counterpoints. Put apricot white with cornflower blue or apple white with coral to gauge the effect.

For a more emphatic statement, look at the pastels which are one degree darker than natural white. Consider some of the cooler tones which are especially suitable for modern or formal settings – and don't forget the classics like cream, magnolia, mist grey and pure brilliant white.

Which should you choose?

**Small, dark rooms** need the enlarging qualities of the palest natural whites. Avoid brilliant white which takes on a tinge of grey where light is limited.

**Cold rooms** which face north or east look warmer with a tint of rose, primrose or apricot.

**Sunny rooms** usually face south or west and welcome the freshness of a hint of apple or lavender.

**Primary colours** require a cool contrast. Pick brilliant white or pale grey.

**Neutral schemes** need toning whites. If the scheme is cool, use brilliant white, apple white or grey. If it contains warmer shades like beige or honey, opt for apricot or barley white, buttermilk or magnolia.

Above: blush pink provides a sympathetic background for the ornaments in this room, emphasizing the colour and detail of the border, plates and flowers.

Right: rose-beige adds warmth to these walls without diminishing the sense of space created by the white paintwork. Decoration is added by the stencil beneath.

Similar shades used for walls and carpet create a most restful setting in this living room. The walls are painted silver grey to picture-rail level to offset the display of paintings, while the french door is stained to match the green-gold shade of the sofa. The ceiling is kept white to reflect the maximum amount of light.

The range of soft, natural whites shows how the colours of the rainbow are muted by the high concentration of white. The basic red, orange, yellow, green and blue become pink, apricot, primrose, apple and sky blue, while neutrals like brown and grey brighten into cream or beige and silver or mist grey. Warmer whites contain a little pink (magnolia) or yellow (buttermilk) while cool pastels such as celadon (grey-green) and azure blue are created with a touch of grey.

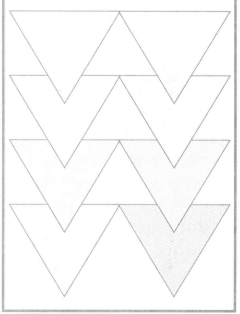

White and ivory make a really effective combination in this small bathroom. White is often used to match bathroom ware but it can cast a chill where light is limited; here ivory is introduced to add warmth. Both are a perfect complement to the cork flooring and natural wood cupboard while the pink lamp over the basin helps to cast a warm glow.

A one-colour scheme relieved by just a splash of yellow. In this stylish setting a variety of angles and materials are cleverly unified – the secret behind this is simply a disciplined use of colour. The materials chosen for the floor and furniture are neutral – marble, glass, and chrome – and the touches of colour are restricted to the bar stools in the kitchen on the right and the painting on the left.

**Decorating with Whites**
- **Texture is important in one-colour schemes. Where a room lacks colour contrast, it's an idea to add rugs and fabrics to impart warmth. Gloss-painted floorboards and furniture will reflect the light to provide extra interest.**
- **Paintwork should be part of the colour scheme, so use a white which relates to the walls when painting the woodwork and radiators.**
- **Ceilings are often best painted in a pale colour to reflect the light, but it needn't be pure brilliant white. A soft white which tones with the walls prevents a harsh contrast, while pastel shades will subtly offset mouldings and decorations which are painted white.**

Think pink – and not just for bedrooms and bathrooms. Let it come out of the closet and into the hall, the living room or the kitchen – pink is too versatile a colour to be shut away upstairs. Pink has a welcoming warmth in the home and it's not a demanding shade like the red to which it's related. Because of its prettiness, pink is more usually associated with feminine colour schemes but its potential is too great to restrict to the boudoir. Its use is more general than you may realize; pink makes an appearance in magnolia (the second most popular paint shade after white), in fawn, and in some shades of peach and apricot. There's a pink that's right for every room: rose-peach warms up a chilly living room, rose-beige looks distinctive in the hall, and cranberry makes a dramatic dining room. A bright pink is surprisingly successful in the kitchen where it offsets the formality of wood or laminate units, while the palest shades like blossom pink are the classic choice for bedrooms.

You may be surprised to learn that the natural contrast to pink is green and not blue (although it does have a close affinity to green); the two are ideal companions in many colour schemes. Other popular partners are lilac, yellow, and the neutrals brown and grey. As pinks vary from those with a blue tinge to those with yellow, it's important to choose co-ordinates which have a similar emphasis unless you have an expert eye for colour.

Left: pink is as at home in the living room as it is in the bedroom. Be positive about it; this room gains warmth from an uncompromisingly bright pink on the walls which complements the softer coral in the upholstery and rug.

Below left: pink meets peach in a dining room where dresser, walls and ceiling are all painted the same shade to increase the sense of space.

Right: deep blush pink creates impact in this narrow hall and is used on the ceiling as well as the walls to make a feature of the cornice.

Below right: palest pink transforms the kitchen into a pretty room. The theme is emphasized by the crockery, festoon blind and stencilled garland.

Rose by any other name may be baby's breath, clover or blush, candyfloss, cerise or raspberry. It may almost be peach (rose-peach), brown (rose-beige) or cream (magnolia): a pink to suit every style of decor and taste. If shocking pink ceilings or carnation walls are not for you, there's a wealth of paler tones to choose from – perfect backgrounds to set off furnishings, fabrics and other details in the deeper pinks.

**Decorating with Pink**
● **Choose a subtle shade of pink with a touch of beige for maximum versatility in living rooms and halls.**
● **Pick up the pink in furnishings such as bedlinen, curtains, cushions and rugs.**
● **Reserve shocking pink and cerise for accessories, or use them to create impact in rooms like the cloakroom where you don't linger for long.**

A north-facing living room can seem chilly. Here, rose-peach on the walls transforms the light into a warm and welcoming glow, complementing perfectly the cream upholstery and beige carpet.

**Decorating with Dark Shades**

• Don't interrupt a dark wall with contrasting doors or mouldings. Paint them to match the colour of the wall and keep to shades of equal depth for carpets, flooring and fitted furniture to create an impression of space.

• Artificial light is especially important in dark rooms. Choose fittings which cast pools of light to illuminate specific areas because general lighting will only make the room seem gloomy. Consider using lights with tungsten halogen lamps which cast a dramatically bright light.

This selection of dramatic settings appears in all the shades of darkness from the lightest grey to charcoal and black, and from midnight blue to violet.

**Grey** is a current favourite and its popularity has ensured that a variety of shades is available from mist to charcoal grey, which is a strong favourite for carpets and furnishings. In theory, grey is the only true neutral as it contains only black and white, but in decorating you'll find shades which have a definite tinge of pink, green, blue or beige. Grey works well with yellow and red, but for a subtler look team it with honey or blue, or opt for a sophisticated scheme of grey, buttermilk and beige.

**Dark blue** has been a popular colour for decorating ever since the ancient Britons covered themselves in woad. Modern Britons are equally attached to dark blues in their wardrobes. Denim blue is a colour for work-wear that's found the world over, thanks to the hardy indigo plant.

Though navy and related shades have always been popular for clothes, they are rarely used in the home, almost exclusively restricted to the front door. Yet navy and royal blues contrast beautifully with peach, they look smart with beige and honey, and with red they're absolutely unbeatable.

**Purple** is a demanding colour that's either in or out of vogue – the last time it was popular in home decoration was the early Seventies when a purple carpet was the last word. If the use of dark blue in the home is limited, purple is even more elusive. Full strength it can certainly be overpowering, but don't overlook the appeal of violet-blue and lilac. As purple is made from equal parts of red and blue, the colours derived from it veer towards one or the other so colour matching can be difficult. If a room scheme includes a fabric which mingles violet with mauve, then both of those shades can be used. A plain lilac, however, is best combined with contrasting colours like primrose and green or a more closely related colour such as pink; or even just

Above: denim moves indoors to cover walls, furniture and ceiling in this stylish bedroom. Pattern has been kept to a minimum and the only contrast comes from the carefully placed areas of red.

Left: warm pine and bamboo furniture is used to counter the charcoal used here for walls and carpet. As any variation in colour would detract from the drama, identical shades are used for both surfaces.

white; matching tones of the same colour is much trickier.

How can you use dark colours in the home? While in most rooms it's usual to try to increase the amount of light by using pale colours to reflect it, you might consider using dark colours to create atmosphere in rooms more frequently lit by artificial light, like the dining room and bedroom. Don't overlook the potential of dark shades for paintwork in place of white or pastels; reversing the normal arrangement of deep walls and light paintwork gives an impact that's especially suited to modern settings. Capitalize on a room that is naturally gloomy and go for a dark, dramatic decor. But don't forget that sombre colours absorb the light, so it's best to reserve these schemes for rooms you relax in rather than those where good illumination is required for reading or work.

Denim, navy, purple and charcoal are all 'saturated' shades, that is, colours which have been darkened by the addition of black or grey. At the deepest end of the scale, the colours become practically black themselves. When the amount of added black is reduced, the colour range brightens. Navy is transformed into royal blue, purple lightens to violet or mauve, while charcoal pales to mist grey or silver.

Above: purple, grey and black combine to form a distinguished setting which shows that dark shades need not be oppressive. Light is reflected by the mirror and white, for contrast, is concentrated on the mantelpiece and in the furnishings. Mouldings are painted to match the walls – white here would look too busy and appear to break up the space. The chrome lamp, table base and metallic picture frames all echo the steely grey which predominates.

Left: the foreground of this all-white room is bathed in soft daylight, and the colours there are 'natural': the green in the cushion, the pale floorboards and the cream leather sofa all appear true. The area of the room which is in shadow has a greyish cast about it.

Below: the cream sofa has a pale orangey look once all the side lamps are lit. The reds are richer than in daylight, while the green in the cushion has lost its brightness. In this mixture of light and shade, most colours are indistinguishable unless in direct light.

Left: the overall tungsten lighting produces a yellowish effect. The red rug looks brighter, so does the red chair at the back of the room. But the green in the cushions now looks washed out and the pale floorboards now appear honey-coloured.

LIGHT ON COLOUR

e all know how some artificial lights seem to flatter us, while others are much harsher and show up every flaw. In the same way, lighting can affect the look of colours in an interior. This is something you need to remember when planning a colour scheme: that colours look different in different types of light.

When we choose colours we tend to evaluate them in daylight. But the amount of daylight in a room varies constantly, as does its intensity and quality. Light is the medium through which we see colour, so, as daylight changes, the colours we see are never really constant, although the changes are often very subtle.

There are two main types of artificial lighting and they both have particular characteristics that alter the appearance of colour. The standard light bulb, known as tungsten filament, produces a light that is close to daylight but slightly yellower; it emphasizes red tones but suppresses blues and greens. Fluorescents, on the other hand, give off a harsh bluish cast that makes colours appear cold and dull, reduces shadows and flattens textures. The newer 'warm' fluorescents are, however, closer to tungsten. Another relatively new development is the tungsten-halogen bulb which produces a whitish light.

How colours appear under these different lights will obviously affect your planning decisions. A paint chart or a furnishing fabric seen in a shop under fluorescent lights will alter perceptibly when you take it home where the lighting is different. Move the sample round the room and look at it at various times of the day, and under artificial lighting at night, before making any final choice.

Look, too, at the way the colours work together. Colour combinations that are perfect in daylight may not work in artificial light. So try to use colours that work well both at night and in the daytime.

A clear yellow, a soft mid-green and a pale pink – this is how we judge the colours of these cushions when we see them in daylight. The whites are white and the cream has only a hint of yellow in it.

Under tungsten light, the yellow looks lighter, the pink has more red in it while the green is duller. Both the white and the cream seem much yellower.

All the warmth has disappeared under the harshness of fluorescent light. The overall effect is colder and bluer – the pink of the cushion now looks almost mauve.

Green is nature's neutral, a foil for the bright blossoms and fruits the plants produce. That's why it is such an adaptable colour in the home, where it combines successfully with every other shade. Forget the maxim 'blue and green should never be seen' – blue is one of the colours which has the most affinity with green (the other is yellow). Blue and green used together create a cool, restful interior while yellow adds warmth and brightness. For contrast, use green with red or tones of pink, peach or violet, or choose green on its own, offset by brilliant white for freshness.

Different greens suit different styles of furnishing. Modern settings ask for leaf green and emerald; traditional interiors favour celadon (grey-green), Wedgewood, forest green and olive. Turquoise, where green and blue combine, has a place in both, but lime, a blend of green and yellow, is an acid shade which can be more difficult to use; team it with lemon or sharp pink to be sure of success. The lively shades of green, such as jade or emerald, work especially well in areas like the kitchen and bathroom. Though officially a cool colour, green has a natural brightness which looks attractive with all shades whether cool or warm. Wherever you decorate with green, you'll increase its impact by adding masses of leafy plants.

Above: soft green, a shade much favoured in the Georgian era, gives a calm, graceful air to this traditional living room.

Above right: dark green makes this window a bold feature. The curtain fabric echoes the colour; walls are cream for contrast.

Right: a vibrant combination of greens: jade jug and basin displayed on a lime washstand; touches of red strike a lively note.

Green has been proved to be the most restful of all hues but it can also be bright and fresh. It's composed from a mixture of yellow and blue, and these two colours appear in its different shades. At the extremes are turquoise and lime, but you'll also find blue in jade and yellow in pistachio. Some variations of green are subtle blends with grey, celadon being one of the most popular.

**Decorating with Green**

• **Decide whether you want to create a bright effect with vivid greens such as jade or lime, or a more tranquil one, using softer or deeper shades such as celadon or forest green.**

• **Don't be afraid to use dark or bright green in kitchens or bathrooms to contrast with white fittings or natural timber units.**

• **Emphasize green by using leafy pot-plants as accessories.**

• **Wicker, wood and cork add texture and** warmth and are green's natural companions.

• **Dark colours absorb light, especially when surfaces are textured. If you plan to use deep green textiles, make sure they don't appear black under artificial light.**

Left: a room with white fittings can take the dramatic contrast of dark walls. Mirrored cupboards make the most of the light.

Above: celadon gives this room a light, airy feeling. Shutters, wicker furniture, cool ceramic tiles and an array of green plants, which highlight the pastel grey-green of the walls, all contribute towards the conservatory-style atmosphere. Both fresh and soothing, green plays an important role here.

Walls and cupboards the colour of clotted cream make a warm and gentle background for this cottage kitchen. The same paint shade used throughout ties the room together and helps to present a united front, while tiles, curtain fabric and tablecloth have been carefully chosen to harmonize.

Gold, a popular colour choice for carpets and curtains, can create a warm and restful atmosphere when used on the walls as this living room shows. The mix of brown and yellow in gold makes it an ideal partner for the rich tones of wood. Curtains with a gold motif on a paler ground give a lift to this mellow scheme.

range and yellow are warm colours which are closely related to each other. They are bright, cheerful hues which create a stimulating environment; neither is easily overlooked! Use clear, citrus colours to add sparkle to dull rooms, but choose paler tones of primrose and apricot for a less demanding background. Deep, rich shades of burnt orange and gold help create a tranquil atmosphere.

**Orange** is the colour that's closest to red. It shares many of red's attributes and at its most intense is best used in small quantities. But orange needn't be day-glo bright. Apricot and peach are both examples of pale orange, while coral and flame occur where orange meets red. Ginger is deep orange; a few shades darker, orange becomes brown. Many colour schemes benefit from a touch of orange in one form or another as it adds warmth to our northern light, whether the scheme is based on autumn colours, blues and greens, or even black and grey.

**Yellow** has an ambivalence which comes from its position between orange and green. It can be a difficult colour to co-ordinate so it's often best to use materials from a single range, where the same dyes are used for a variety of items. It's also important to examine yellows in both natural and artificial light in the room where they will be used, to avoid clashes between gold and lemon yellows. Yellow is held to be one of the three primary colours because it cannot be made by mixing any other hues. (In some systems used by artists and scientists, however, green replaces yellow as the third primary.) Yellow is the lightest of the primary colours and its light-reflecting qualities are increased (though its impact is reduced) as it pales to primrose. With the addition of green and grey yellow forms mustard, and with orange and brown turns to gold. Gold is a decorating classic, one of the most popular colours for carpets and furnishings, that adds warmth to any setting.

Left: acid yellow needs accessories in strong colours, like scarlet and french blue, to balance the effect.

Below: yellow and white is a fresh and cheerful combination. Here the ceiling and dresser top have been stained to match the cupboards and reveal the grain of the wood. Beams and chairs are painted white for emphasis.

Next to red in the spectrum come orange and yellow, which share its qualities of power and warmth. The popularity of orange fluctuates with fashion. Bright orange was much in vogue 20 years ago, but the current emphasis is on easy-to-live-with tones of peach and apricot. Orange shades into brown at the darker end of the scale. Yellow is a perennial favourite. Whether full strength or as primrose, lemon, Chinese yellow, mustard or gold, its ability to reflect light while adding warmth makes it particularly valuable in interior decorating.

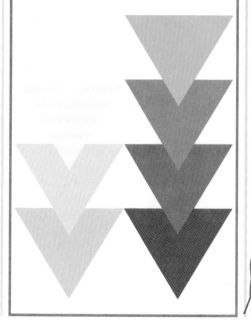

**Decorating with Orange and Yellow**
● Use yellow and orange in rooms with a cool (north or east-facing) aspect to add warmth.
● Choose paler shades (peach and primrose) to increase the amount of light, darker ones (brown and gold) for a restful atmosphere.
● Take care to avoid clashes between lemon and golden yellows, and between pink and yellow shades of orange.
● Brilliant white makes a refreshing contrast to the intensity of yellow and orange.

**Decorating with Peach**
- Choose peach to give warmth to chilly rooms which face north or east, and also in those where there is restricted light.
- Pick apricot or blends of peach and pink for pretty, feminine schemes.
- Yellowy peach or orange versions look attractive in bold modern rooms.
- Blue contrasts with both peach and orange. Choose azure or grey-blue for use with coral or pink-peach, aqua or cornflower to team with apricot.

Right: stronger than peach, but softer than pure orange, terracotta is a lovely warm colour for floors, whether painted or tiled.
Far right: with its air of the orient, this living room calls for clear, warm-coloured walls. Here, a deep peach provides the perfect setting.

Take a dash of orange, dilute it with white and blend it with with pink, What's the result? Peach, which is currently (and with good reason) one of furnishing's top favourites. Because it's pale, peach is easy to live with and makes the most of light and space. Because it's next to orange and red, peach adds warmth, necessary in so many north or east-facing rooms or those made gloomy by limited light. And because it's pastel, it's a delicate shade, ideal for pretty or traditional schemes.

There's more than one version of peach of course. Think how the fruit from which it takes its name turns from yellow to pink and that will give you some idea of its versatility. Yellow or orange tints look good in modern settings as do darker shades such as soft terracotta, which are also perfect for country-style schemes. Step up the pink and peach becomes coral, salmon or flame – warm, lively colours that combine the qualities of orange, pink and red.

What we normally think of as peach, however, is the more uniform colour of its

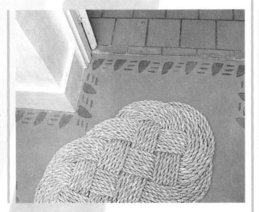

sister fruit, the apricot. And what better to put with peach, or apricot, than cream? Softer than white, cream contains a hint of yellow which makes it the ideal companion for one of the softest and most versatile of all the pastels. Wherever they are used, peach and cream form a combination that's easy to live with and always in style.

Left: here is a room that uses the theme of peaches and cream to great effect. Pale peach on the walls makes the most of available light and adds a gentle warm glow. The creamy brown and soft terracotta colours in the large floor rug are both close relatives to peach and provide many of the colour cues in the rest of the decor. Doors are painted a toning light beige; soft furnishings and accessories play on variations of peach, terracotta and cream.

Peach is pale orange, and draws on its neighbours on the colour wheel to produce tones like coral or salmon which contain a high concentration of pink (a version of red) or yellow. Peach is created by adding white to orange and, like the other pastels is less demanding, and absorbs less light, than the pure hue from which it is derived. As one of the warmer pastels, it is especially useful in home decorating.

# COLOUR AND PERSONALITY

**R**ed indicates that you're adventurous, ambitious and passionate. As red is closely associated with the sun it is not suprising that a preference for this colour suggests a fiery temperament and a zest for living life to the full. However, it can also mean that you might have a somewhat tempestuous nature; certainly life will never be dull around you.

**B**lue represents peace, tranquility and wisdom.If you are drawn to blue, you like calm, and you're loyal too; you are unlikely to trade friendship for position. It suggests a mature and prudent attitude to life. On the debit side, you may sometimes appear to be cool, withdrawn, and reluctant to commit yourself.

**O**range is a less fiery version of red. Midway between the two warm primaries, it tempers the passion and force of red with the cheerfulness of yellow. It points to a sunny, luxury-loving nature. Brown, the darker version of orange, represents contentment and security though too great a liking for brown may indicate a tendency to depression.

**P**ink is not just for little girls. Like blue, it has a calming effect and suggests a warm and relaxed personality. Too great an emphasis on pink may indicate an undeveloped personality, someone who looks at life through 'rose-coloured glasses'.

**P**urple is the colour of royalty and is therefore associated with such noble traits as love of truth, justice and right living. On the reverse side, it can indicate self-importance and a lack of realism. Violet, as it is officially known in the colour wheel, also lays stress on spirituality and meditation.

**G**reen indicates a well-balanced personality with a tendency towards conservative, and even sometimes rather self-satisfied, attitudes. Yet green is also the colour of youth, hope and a joyous, rich life and these traits may be associated with you. Green can also indicate a lack of maturity in some areas – and you've heard about being 'green with envy'.

**Y**ellow is the colour of optimism. Though less demanding than red, it shares its attributes as a stimulating, sunny colour. If yellow is your favourite, you are likely to be cheerful, and happy-go-lucky. However, it may also indicate a tendency to be frivolous and superficial, an unwillingness to take life seriously.

● Colour can affect us psychologically, making us feel happy or depressed, anxious or relaxed, and even physically raising or depressing the blood pressure.

● It can also change our perception of size and of time. The colours we choose to live with tells more than we may like to think about our personalities.

Red is the first colour primitive societies name after they have distinguished black and white. That's an indication of its power, for red is the colour of fire and of blood. The first colour of the rainbow and the most powerful of the primaries, red has almost magical qualities; it can actually make your heart beat faster! It's also an enlarging colour – objects seem bigger if they are painted red, which is why it's often used in packaging.

In the home, its effect can be rather different. On the positive side, red is the colour of vitality, adding warmth and impact to any setting. However, red can dominate, overpowering every other colour – it stands out noticeably against blue and yellow in a room decorated in primary colours. A little red goes a long way and may seem oppressive used over a large area. Although red walls enclose and add warmth to a large and draughty hall, they may appear to crowd and overwhelm the occupants in a small, intimate room.

Below: this crimson hall makes such an impact that there's no need for any other colour or decoration.

Right: glossy red walls give this otherwise simply-furnished dining room an impression of richness.

Scarlet is only one of the reds; flame is red plus orange, terracotta is red blended with brown, and with black red becomes burgundy. Matt surfaces soften the impact of red but its qualities are emphasized by shiny surfaces (red lacquer, much favoured by the Chinese, and red gloss paint are traditional favourites for furniture and doors). When choosing carpets and curtains in red, remember that synthetic fabrics are brighter in colour than natural ones like wool and cotton. Note, too, that red is one of the colours that are prone to fade, so line red curtains and protect upholstery from direct sunlight.

The most dynamic of all colours, red demands an instant response. Use scarlet to attract attention; choose a darker shade, like terracotta or burgundy, if you prefer less intense colour; or consider flame-red to add warmth. Red is close to purple and orange and merges with them to make magenta and flame. Add white and they change to fuchsia and coral. Though they're so different, pink and red are variations on the same theme.

**Decorating with Red**

● Red walls appear to reduce space, so reserve them for large areas, such as halls, or rooms where you want to create a sense of drama.

● Red is a stimulating colour so be sparing with vivid patterns on furnishings and accessories. They will compete with the colour for attention and the effect may be confusing.

● Red increases the apparent size and importance of objects, so use it with care.

Top: studies should stimulate! See how red doors and accessories perk up this home office.

Above: red adds warmth and brightness while creamy yellow is used to reflect light in this dark kitchen.

Flame-red ceiling and walls seem to give warmth to this large bedroom, which might look chilly otherwise. Light from the window is reflected by the pale carpet in a reversal of the usual combination of white ceiling and dark floor.

Right: this fresh and attractive combination of bright blue and white belies blue's reputation as a cold colour.

Below: blue not only cheers up the storage area in this contemporary scheme; it also acts as a perfect foil for the silver-grey background and the black and charcoal furniture.

**Decorating with Blue**

● Blue schemes can create a peaceful and serene setting, but take care using paler tones or they may appear too cool.

● Combine blue with tones such as pink and peach for warmth.

● Reserve related schemes of blue and green, grey or violet for sunny south- or west-facing rooms.

● Pick up the blue used in a room scheme in decorative china; plates look especially pretty hung on walls.

● Use blue paint to unite an assortment of furniture – chest, cupboard and headboard for example, or dining table and chairs.

● Use blues with greens and mauves of equal depth, or 'value',

to create the most restful schemes.

● Blue and black can be a striking combination. Look for deep cornflower or electric blues with maximum intensity to balance the effect.

● Warm a blue room with natural wood furniture. For cool sophistication, substitute glass and chrome.

Above: casually colour-washed wall and matching mirror frame and chest of drawers are integrated by the use of one paint colour. Gauloise blue was chosen to go with the bedcover and give instant co-ordination to this modest room.

Right: blue can have a calming influence in busy areas like halls. White woodwork adds sparkle and a mirror is placed to reflect the light. Interest is added by the patterned cloth, which combines warm red with the same blue and white.

Calm and serene or cold and un-welcoming? Blue is the coolest colour in the spectrum but it is also considered the most peaceful. This ambiguity is echoed in the nature of the colour itself. The sea and sky seem blue to us, but this appearance is in fact a reflection of blue light on a transparent substance – in eyes as well as air and water.

Many people name blue as their favourite primary because they feel more at ease with it than with vivid yellow or red. It's a colour that's rarely out of fashion for long because it suits every complexion, but it can be easier to wear than to use in the home. People seem to complain of the cold sooner in a room painted blue than in one decorated in warmer colours, so when you are planning a blue scheme it's wise to add a contrasting colour such as gold, pink, or apricot – a version of orange which is blue's true complement – which will provide warm accents throughout the room.

There are so many versions of blue that it can be difficult to establish which is the 'true blue' – or which is the most pleasant to live with. At its extremes, blue blends with purple to form lavender or merges with green to make turquoise and jade. Mixed with black, blue becomes navy and mingled with grey produces azure. In the centre is cornflower or Alice blue, a bright and sunny colour which looks pretty with cream and apricot. Pale blues can be difficult to use – they are the tones most likely to appear cold – but they look delicate mixed with lilac, pale green and bone or white and they make good contrasts with textured materials in natural warm browns like timber, cane and cork. Strong blues look effective on furniture, whether painted or upholstered, and work well on the walls and ceilings of bedrooms and dining rooms where they seem both impressive and calm.

Blue is a host of colours wrapped up in one. It can be as bright as cornflowers or forget-me-nots or as pale as azure or ice. It turns lavender when mixed with violet, and turquoise when blended with green, its neighbours in the spectrum of colours. The darkest blues, such as navy, can act in the same way as more neutral colours to define a scheme, while smoky shades provide adaptable colours especially suitable for background use on walls, carpets or furnishings, making an effect that's more colourful than grey, more subtle than brighter blues.

**Decorating with Browns**

- **Mix brown and beige with silver, black and charcoal for a very sophisticated effect.**
- **Use dark brown with care – it swallows the light.**
- **Inject a little variety into neutral beige schemes. A mix of warm textures like wool and wood plus a gleam of polished steel adds interest.**
- **Remember that dark brown carpets will show every speck.**
- **Brighten up beige and brown schemes by adding accents of orange or blue for contrast.**

Full of natural goodness, the earth colours range from dark chocolate to cream. Honey-beige and tan come in between. Look at the wide scope of timber colours: red browns include mahogany and rosewood, yellow browns echo pine and maple; green browns resemble walnut. Made paler, brown becomes a neutral beige, while russet and tan remind us of brown's proximity to orange.

Left: red-brown walls echo the warm glow of the polished shelves and fire surround.

Below: creamy-beige walls contribute to the restful mood of this living room.

Above: chocolate and tan are teamed to give the traditional brown study a fashionable

slant. Earthy colours predominate here to make a pleasant workplace.

Two contrasts – beige and grey plus modern furnishings in a traditional setting – make this a most striking scheme. The different colours are confined to separate areas, beige in the background and grey in front, for maximum effect.

ountry colours like brown and beige had a field day (what else?) in the Seventies. Then came the grey revival which dislodged beige from its place as the most popular neutral. Autumn shades went into abeyance as fashion emphasized Memphis colours like citrus yellow, turquoise and coral, and turned to black in place of brown. Currently we're seeing new ways of using old favourites because beige and brown are too useful to neglect – they are now used not just for a rural feel, but also to produce city-smart schemes designed to show that grey and black are not essential to achieve style.

Brown has no 'official' place in the colour spectrum, which is why it is often thought to be neutral. In fact, it's a derivative of orange, as the brighter tans and russets clearly show. Dark browns range from virtually black to those which place the emphasis on grey. Beige is pale brown, sometimes with a hint of pink, green or yellow, and should be blended with care, taking into account the different hues on which the tones are based. For contrast, add accents of brown's opposite, which is blue. Consider putting navy blue with russet, or sky blue with chocolate, for example, or mix French navy with beige.

Black also works well with brown and white in a liquorice allsorts combinaton of colours – and there's no rule which says that beige can't be used with grey. These schemes not only help to co-ordinate new with existing furnishings but challenge traditional ideas of decoration. Because brown is the colour of natural wood it will always have a place in our homes; we need to be equally flexible in the ways we use it.

Below: white walls and black paintwork form a contrast that's set off by the warm tones of polished wood flooring and furniture.

Right: in a confined space, red and white create a dramatic impact against a background of solid, glossy black.

Below right: with a subtle grey balancing the stronger tones, the simplicity of this hallway area is given a cool elegance.

he dramatic contrast of black and white makes an exceptionally stylish decorating solution.

A room painted in black and white always has a strong, distinctive identity, but it need not appear stark or comfortless. The overall mood depends on the shape and size of the room itself and the balance of tones throughout; this can be varied in subtle ways according to the function of the room and the details of furnishings, ornaments and other objects which it contains.

To make the most of an open, light space, choose clean white walls framed by glossy black paintwork. Both elements capitalize on the available light and respond to the addition of warm or cool colours as a balancing factor. Black makes a virtue of an enclosed or restricted space, such as a bathroom or small den, emphasizing its privacy and lending itself to decorative touches of colour and detail in curtains, cushions, pretty lamps and other accessories.

The neutrality of black and white can be exploited by the addition of bright, primary colours, cool, subtle blues and greys or the warm brown tones of natural wood, cane and similar materials. In fact, this is an endlessly versatile colour choice, adaptable to both traditional and modern furnishing styles.

Colour is the vital element in design, bringing spaces, shapes and patterns to life. This powerful potential can be intimidating when it comes to choosing colours to live with; many people lack confidence to make the most of colour, falling back on safe or neutral shades. However, there are basic principles which enable you to exploit colour without letting it get out of hand.

The colour wheel (far right) shows the relationships of pure colours. At the centre are the primary colours – red, blue and yellow. Mixtures of any two of these form the secondary colours – orange (red and yellow), green (blue and yellow), violet (blue and red) – which occupy the second band of the wheel. Combinations of primary and secondary colours form the outer ring, providing red-violet and red-orange, yellow-orange and yellow-green, blue-violet and blue-green.

Schemes for harmonious or contrasting colours can be selected according to the position of colours on the wheel. Harmonious schemes derive from colours close together on the wheel – yellow and orange, for example, or yellow through shades of yellow-green to green. Contrasting schemes derive from colours opposite one another on the wheel, called complementary colours. Contrasts of opposing primary and secondary colours – red and green, yellow and violet, blue and orange – are vivid, even brash. The selection of opposing mixed hues from the outer band of the wheel echoes these contrasts but with a softer effect because the colours are more complex. Harmonies and contrasts can be devised that are bright and bold or subtle and muted, according to personal preference.

The inherent qualitites of different

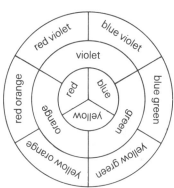

The colour wheel shows the relationships of colours, adjacent and harmonious or opposite and contrasting. Warm, advancing colours fall on the red/orange side of the spectrum, while the receding blues and greens are cool.

colours can be used to create optical effects in a room. The apparent warmth or coolness of a colour is demonstrated by the colour wheel. Red and orange hues, moving towards violet on one side and yellow on the other, are warm, advancing colours which create a sense of closeness and comfort. Blues and greens tend to be

cool and distancing, giving the appearance of making space rather than drawing it in. Yellow and violet vary in their effects; sunshine yellow is warm and welcoming while fresh lemon is cool; violet derives its effect from the balance of its component colours, red and blue, and thus warm or cool.

Uninhibited, bright colours have a special appeal for children. This entertaining room scheme successfully employs the primary colours.

THE COLOUR WHEEL

# SUCCESS WITH

## SCHEMES

The real art of interior decorating is knowing how to handle colour. It is about choosing the exact shade of red to use with a clear midnight blue, judging how much flamingo pink you need to liven up an all-white scheme without destroying its sophisticated look, and which shades of green to mix together.

Colour is the single most important ingredient in decorating. It can transform the whole atmosphere of your home more quickly and cheaply than anything else. You can use colour to change a dingy room into a light fresh one, to disguise awkwardly shaped spaces or to make a small room seem larger – all in the time it takes to paint the walls.

Making the decisions, however, can be a formidable task – after all, there is an enormous range of colours to choose from. The human eye can distinguish over ten million different colours and there are over 500 shades in the Dulux Matchmaker range alone. The choice can appear to be overwhelming.

The key to successful colour schemes is knowing which colours to put together. Fortunately, this is a skill that can be learnt without difficulty.

Above: a perfectly balanced scheme in pale blue and yellow. Opposite: this kitchen is gently coloured for a charming fresh look.

It all becomes much clearer once you've grasped the basic principles of colour and how colours relate to each other. Turn back and study the colour wheel on page 29 – it only takes a few minutes to understand and it is an important decorating tool. If you want to create a calm, harmonious atmosphere, choose colours that are close together on the wheel, while livelier, contrasting schemes are made up of colours opposite each other.

Or you can choose a scheme made up of various tones of one colour, adding a little contrast colour for interest.

Before you decide on a particular colour, work out exactly what kind of effect you want to create – it could be light and airy, soft and homely, calm or cheerful; it might be rustic or formal, or modern and sophisticated. Now list the colours that convey that look. Cool greys and pale yellows, for example, create an up-to-the-minute sophisticated atmosphere, warm reds and pinks give a cosy, homely feel.

You can also train yourself to observe the way colours are combined in nature and in art. Take a bunch of pink roses, for example – there will be at least three or four different pinks in the petals; stamens of a pale mustardy yellow; a stem of mossy green and leaves a darker green, glossy on top and matt, almost silvery, underneath. Or think of the variety of reds, golds, oranges, pale greens and yellows found in a pile of autumn leaves. Paintings are another wonderful source of inspiration – start with the work of Monet and Matisse, both of whom were marvellous colourists.

Keep a notebook with you and jot down any colour combinations you come across that strike you as particularly pleasing. Similarly, before you discard old colour magazines, tear out any pictures whose colours you respond to and file them. Use these for inspiration as a starting point – some of the combinations may be suitable for a whole room, others could be used in a fabric or as accent colours.

Gradually, you will develop an eye for colour and you will be able to start choosing and mixing it with confidence and flair.

Planning a colour scheme – choosing colours for walls and floor, fabric for curtains and upholstery, as well as all the extra finishing touches – can be great fun, although for some it may also seem a rather daunting prospect. However, once you have a basic understanding of colour and a systematic approach to it, plus some of the tricks of the trade used by professional interior designers, you will find the whole process of planning a scheme a lot easier and much more enjoyable.

Before you even begin to think about specific colours, have a good look around the room to be decorated. Write down what you like about it and what you don't like. How much natural light does it get? Is it too small or an awkward shape? Think about its structural condition and whether any essential repairs and alterations are needed. Are the walls, ceiling and floor surfaces in good enough condition? Ensure

The Dulux Colour Tester with its handy built-in brush is the ideal way to try out colours you want to use on walls, next to carpets, curtains and furnishings – for a perfect match.

Gathering samples is the best way to arrive at a successful colour scheme. Collect paint chips, swatches of fabric and carpet samples.

| DATE | PRESENT STATE | REPAIRS/ALTERATIONS | DECORATIVE TREATMENT |
|------|---------------|---------------------|----------------------|
| LIGHTING | Central light only | Replace with wall lights on dimmer switch | Add uplights and table lamps |
| ELECTRICITY | One wall socket | Put new sockets in each corner. Add TV socket | Check out hardware - brass, brushed steel or white? |
| HEATING | Gas heater in fireplace | Restore fireplace, add two radiators under windows | Add coal-flame effect fire |
| WALLS | Shabby paper | Strip and line | Paint with emulsion, stipple and add border below ceiling |
| CEILING | Cracked | Line with paper | Paint with emulsion |
| FLOOR | Floor boards - fair condition | Strip, sand, seal and varnish | Buy rugs |
| WINDOWS | Peeling paint | Strip and repaint | Roman blinds initially later add curtains |
| DOORS | Undistinguished | Strip to original pine | Varnish and replace hardware |
| ACCESSORIES | No storage facilities or pictures | Fit glass shelves in recesses | Remount old prints |

you have an adequate number of power points and consider the type of lighting you want. Think about the storage you need and the kind of furniture you own.

From this information you can make a checklist of work to be done, dividing it into repairs/alterations and decorative treatment. This is a good way of making sure you don't forget important details, such as getting older properties rewired before the walls are painted. And it enables you to work out how much everything will cost and what you should spend your money on first. Fortunately, colour is the one item that costs very little – it's only the price of a tin of paint.

Now it's on to choosing the colours. The first step is to establish a starting point from which to work.

You may have a fitted carpet or a sofa that you can't afford – or don't want – to change. In that case, you need to identify the colours it contains and then plan around these.

It's more difficult if you're planning the scheme from scratch. The first thing most interior designers do when they meet new clients is to ask a series of questions to establish what their favourite colours are and which ones they dislike, and what kind of atmosphere is preferred – cool and harmonious, for instance, or warm, welcoming and cosy.

It's worth thinking about each of your favourite colours in turn – why you like it, how it appears in nature, what sort of mood it conveys and all the different versions of it. Then try and imagine it on the walls of your room. If it is too overbearing or too pale, perhaps it would look better in curtains or on a cushion. From there, you can work out which other colours go well with it.

If you have an idea of the atmosphere you want to convey, base your scheme around the colours that convey that mood – for instance, cool pastels and whites create an airy, spacious look, while reds and pinks add warmth.

Once you have decided on the colours you want to include, start collecting samples – a piece of the sofa fabric or a square of the carpet, samples of wood to match the furniture or floorboards, paint charts, coloured wools, wallpaper and so on.

It's important to choose from samples of the real thing – a swatch of fabric or a paint chip, for example – rather than printed images in catalogues which will vary slightly in colour from the actual items.

Play around with the samples until you fix on the basic scheme you feel happiest with. Then make a sample board – one of the tricks interior designers use – by mounting your selection on cardboard so you can judge how the colours, textures and patterns work together. It will give you an idea of how the final scheme will look.

Don't rush off to buy everything yet. Take your time. Leave the sample board in the room to be decorated for a few days. Look at it in different lighting conditions; in daylight, in shadow and under artificial lights – colours change according to the quality and intensity of illumination.

It is quite difficult to imagine what the room will look like when it's been painted, so it's a good idea to buy a small tester pot of the colour you have chosen and try it out on a test patch first. Then you can see how the whole room will look and how the light affects the colour.

Left: the bedroom has been delicately warmed with soft peach vinyl matt on walls offset by woodwork painted in white Satinwood. A rose pink quilt echoes the warm theme while a soft aqua and white striped bedcover adds a stylish touch and flatters the background. Aqua is an excellent cool colour to contrast with peach, being its opposite on the colour wheel with a similar tonal value. The floor has been given an individual touch with apricot white Satinwood, thinned and rubbed in for a subtle effect, creating an appealing link with the colour of the walls.

One of the most exciting things about working out a colour scheme is that you can make the same room appear completely different simply by changing the colours. A deep pink, for instance, will have a cosy look while a sea green is cooler and more sophisticated.

This is perfectly illustrated by these three very successful – and very different – schemes chosen for a loft bedroom belonging to a teenage girl.

The main problem with the room is the fact that it has only one window – the wrong treatment here could easily make the atmosphere dark and oppressive. The obvious solution is to use light fresh colours to convey spaciousness. This approach is used in two of the schemes,

while in the third the walls are sponged (see page 113) blue over blue for a cloudy effect that creates interesting texture as well as producing a cool, airy setting.

Another difficulty was how to deal with the sloping ceiling with its exposed wooden beams – an awkward feature to treat decoratively. Continuing the wall treatment over the ceiling has the effect of increasing the feeling of height; in one of the schemes the beams have been emphasized, in keeping with the cottagey look.

Each of these different schemes was designed to achieve a particular effect: warm and relaxing, country cottage-style, cool and harmonious.

Every colour evokes a definite response – red spells danger; it also means fire and warmth. Yellow is sunshine, white is cool

and pure. Colours fall naturally into two groups. If you want to create a cool, calm atmosphere, choose from the greens, blues and blue-greens – the colours associated with cold running water and mossy banks. Think of fire and sunlight and you automatically see reds, pinks, oranges and yellows – the colours on the opposite half of the colour wheel (see page 29).

Patterns and texture also convey moods. Small dainty patterns are traditionally associated with the countryside – this type is used in the cottagey look opposite. In the cool scheme however, soft stripes and an abstract pattern are just right for the airy, relaxed effect that's required.

As you can see, once you identify the look you want to create, the colours almost seem to choose themselves.

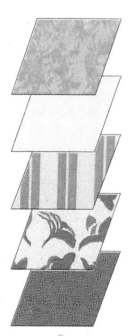

Left: cool and fresh, this harmonious scheme is based around blues and greens. For a gentle cloudy effect, a lovely mid-blue shade, has been delicately sponged over forget-me-not-blue walls, making an interesting texture. Magnolia woodwork has a freshening effect. Fabrics are a mixture of plains – in rough woven mid-blue and mid-green – and patterns. The blue stripes come in two . different scales and are balanced with plenty of white.

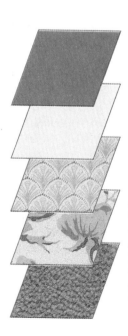

Right: rose white walls and matching bedlinen in palest pink team beautifully with the delicately patterned pink and green quilt and curtains garlanded with flowers for a soft feminine look. The furniture is painted to match the walls, and its beading picked out in deep peach. Although the look is simple, comfort hasn't been sacrificed – creamy beige carpet provides warmth and a texture contrast with the rough woven tablecloth.

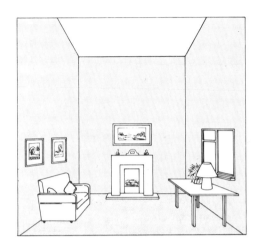

Painting a ceiling white or a light tint has the effect of making the room appear taller than it is because the surface seems further away.

A ceiling that is painted a dark colour or shade will look lower than it is in reality. The effect is caused by 'advancing' colours.

By continuing the dark ceiling colour down to picture-rail level, you can 'lower' a tall room even further.

Once you have learnt some visual tricks with colour, it is possible to alter the apparent proportions of a room. For instance, you can make a small room appear larger, a big barn-like space look much smaller and more homely or a narrow hallway seem wider simply by the clever use of colour and tone.

Tone describes the lightness or darkness, or tonal value, of a colour, from its weakest version to its strongest. A good illustration of how tone works is a black and white photograph in which a coloured image has been converted into tones of black, from black and grey to almost white.

Tints are tones of a colour to which white has been added; shades are tones of a colour which have been darkened with black or grey, or are mixed with another closely related colour.

We have already seen how the colours in the spectrum can be divided into two opposite groups: warm and cool. The effects these groups have on the apparent proportions of a room are opposite too.

Reds, yellows and oranges, as well as creating a warm, cosy atmosphere, appear to bring surfaces closer and are known as advancing colours. Dark tones, or shades,

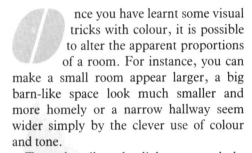

A wall painted in a light tint or a cool colour will recede, making it appear further away than it actually is.

have a similar effect.

Cool colours – blues, violets and greens – and light tones, or tints, have the opposite effect. They make surfaces appear further away than they really are and are known as receding colours.

Paint the ceiling in an advancing colour if the room is high and you want to make it seem lower. You can increase the effect by continuing the ceiling colour down to picture rail level; it also helps to have a floor covering in a similar colour.

A wall that is painted in an advancing

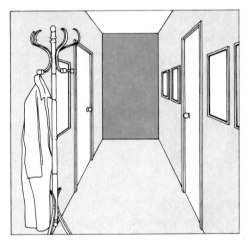

A wall painted in a dark shade or a warm colour will advance, making it seem closer than it really is, useful for decorating the end walls of narrow halls.

colour, or in a dark tone or shade, will appear to be closer than it really is. Given the opposite treatment it will appear further away.

And if you want to create the effect of heightening the ceiling, paint it white or a very light colour, which also increases the amount of reflected light.

Small rooms should be decorated in the palest, lightest colours – receding colours that make the surfaces appear more distant – so they look bigger than they really are and have a more spacious feeling.

Left: the blue wall in this kitchen seems closer than it really is because it's painted in a dark shade. This is emphasized by the pale colours of the bedroom beyond, which make this room seem further away.

Below: white floor and walls retain a sense of space here; but to prevent a barn-like feeling in the room, the ceiling is painted a darkish shade of blue, which has the effect of lowering it optically.

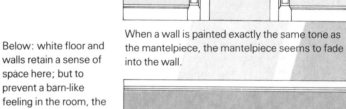

When a wall is painted exactly the same tone as the mantelpiece, the mantelpiece seems to fade into the wall.

When the wall is painted a different, darker, tone than the mantelpiece, the mantelpiece stands out by contrast.

**Effects with Colour**
- You can alter the apparent proportions of a room simply by using colour and tone.
- Tone describes the depth of a colour.
- Shades are tones darkened with black or grey; tints are tones lightened with white.
- Warm advancing colours appear to bring surfaces closer.
- Cool – or receding – colours make surfaces seem further away.
- To make a ceiling seem higher, paint it a light tint; a darker shade will lower it.
- Paint small rooms in pale colours so they seem bigger; do the opposite to reduce space.

One of the simplest and most successful ways of creating an interesting colour scheme is to use two or three, or more, colours that lie next to each other on the colour wheel – peach, pink, apricot and orange are just one example; green, blue-green, aquamarine and sky blue are another.

These types of related colour schemes are called blends, or harmonious schemes, because all the colours are comfortably combined and well balanced, and no two jar or clash. You can choose colours from any one portion of the colour wheel, whether warm or cool, or a combination of both, and the overall effect will be restful and soothing; the degree of harmony created depends on how closely the colours are related.

The scheme will be more pleasing if no two colours are used in equal quantities – it is much more interesting to vary them.

An important point to consider when you are putting a harmonious scheme together is the tonal balance between colours; use it to give depth and lightness

Above: a successful mix of tones makes this green and blue scheme work. The wonderful deep greeny-turquoise ceiling has been lacquered for a highly reflective finish. The cupboards and shelves, stained a mid-greeny blue, stand out against the palest green walls, while sofa and rug are in a strong blue-green.

Right: neutral colours are good mixers. The soft creamy beige on the walls of this living room contains a hint of pink. It gently links the honey-coloured wood floor and rich golden brown sofa with the pale yellow door. Notice how the yellow is repeated in the lampshade over the table. Crisp white woodwork and ceiling keep the scheme looking fresh.

**Harmonious Effects**

● Closely related colours – those that lie next to each other on the spectrum – are called blends, or harmonious colours.

● Using these related colours is one of the easiest ways to colour scheme successfully.

● The overall effect of these schemes is restful and soothing. Add interest by varying the amount of each colour used.

● It is best to use different tones of colours, mixing dark, light and mid-tones with pure colours.

● You can also create these schemes by using tints and shades of just one colour.

● Most harmonious schemes, especially if based on one colour, need some accent colour to add life. Restrict primary colours to accents as they tend to be overwhelming within a scheme.

to the scheme. Sometimes the pastel tones are so pale they appear almost as neutrals beside their stronger cousins. Try to use different intensities of the colours, mixing lighter and darker tones with the mid-tones – for example, pale pink and deep apricot combined with a soft shade of raspberry. And it's a good idea to restrict primary colours to accents otherwise they will destroy the balance of the scheme.

It is even easier to create harmonious schemes using tones of a single colour, from its lightest tint to its darkest shade. After all, there are hundreds of different versions of every colour you might choose – think of the number of blues available in embroidery silks, for instance, or the variety of pinks and reds in the sunset or the tones of green on a vegetable stall. When you're creating this sort of scheme, include tints and shades from all parts of the range so that there is a gentle transition from one to the next.

Sometimes a harmonious scheme using variations on a single colour can turn out to be rather lifeless. The answer is to add a little accent colour – it could be a strong primary or a contrasting colour from the opposite side of the colour wheel – which will help add interest.

Above: blue and green is one of the most popular combinations for related colour schemes. But it need never be boring, as the two examples on these pages show. The tones used in this bedroom are of similar weight but there's more blue than green, which balances the look. The touches of pink add welcome zest.

At one time or another, most of us have despaired of deciding on a colour and have painted every surface in sight either white or an off-white. This is actually a flexible approach because you can add a bit of life to the room by using colour in easily changed accessories.

These small amounts of colour introduced for emphasis are known as accent colours. Accents are about contrast – light against dark, cool colours against warm ones, pure colour against weaker tone. They are a useful way of livening up both harmonious and monochromatic, schemes.

A monochromatic colour scheme is easy to handle. It features a single basic colour or combines different tonal versions of the same colour. This can be used in its pure form and/or with tones. To save such a scheme from being boring, you need to add visual interest by varying textures (see pages 42-43). And a small amount of an accent is essential to anchor the scheme – a black table light in an all-white room, for instance.

Although any colour can be used in a monochromatic scheme, most interiors benefit from the addition of a neutral to emphasize details – for example, an all-blue room with pale blue walls looks fresher and more balanced with white woodwork, while small touches of contrasting accent colours – a yellow or soft orange cushion, perhaps – enliven it.

Only use a few accents in one room, otherwise they'll take over and the balance will be destroyed.

Left: tone on tone. The very light orange-beige walls play up the soft burnt orange of the chimney breast and woodwork. The neutral furniture blends in well. Accessories in sharp blue – orange's complementary colour – lift the scheme, as do the warm pinks and clear oranges in the paintings.

Left: the red banister brings out the difference in the greys used here – steel grey blinds, silvery carpet, deep blue-grey walls and dark gloss-painted balustrades.

**Accent on Colour**
● **Small amounts of colour added for emphasis and contrast are known as accents.**
● **They are a useful way of livening up both harmonious and monochromatic, or single colour schemes.**
● **To achieve a monochromatic scheme, use one colour throughout or combine different tones of one colour.**
● **Handle accents with care; only use a few in any room or they will take over and upset the balance of colour in the scheme.**

A bold turquoise accents rather than camouflages a radiator and turns it into a fun feature.

Below: this brilliant red with a stylish touch of black in it works perfectly with the very soft mid-blue, and both colours seem far removed from their brash primary origins. The combination of the red's gloss-painted texture and the matt blue walls subtly reinforces the contrast between these two colours.

Below right: orange and blue are opposite one another on the colour wheel. Orange is made up equally of two primaries – red and yellow – but it makes an even more vibrant partner to blue than either of these.

**Contrasting Effects**
- A contrasting scheme is made up of opposing colours on the colour wheel.
- These schemes are always more dramatic than harmonious ones, but trickier to put together successfully.
- The pairs of contrast colours, known as complementaries, can be used in their various tints and shades as well as in pure form. It's important to vary the amounts and the strengths of colours for success.

You can create a very dramatic effect by using a contrasting scheme made up of colours that are opposite each other on the colour wheel – blue and yellow, for example, or red and green. These pairs of colours are known as 'complementaries'.

Contrasting colour schemes are much more exciting than harmonious, or blended, ones – even when the former feature the various tones and shades of the complementaries, and not just the pure colours. The most vibrant schemes of all are those where one primary colour is used with an opposite secondary colour – blue and orange, red and green, yellow and purple. You see these in advertisements designed to stimulate and catch the eye.

But these high-contrast schemes are almost impossible to live with. You need to tone down one or all of the colours, or separate them with a related colour or a neutral. White is excellent because it accentuates the colours.

When planning a contrasting scheme for a room, the most important thing to remember is to vary the amounts and strengths of the complementary colours, breaking them up with neutrals, and make sure that no one colour dominates.

## Texture and Pattern

- Texture and pattern are a subtle way of adding visual interest.
- Texture is about the feel of a material to the touch and what its surface looks like.
- Warm textures have rough, non-reflective surfaces; cool ones are usually smooth, shiny and cold.
- If you're using pattern, consider scale carefully; its size can affect the apparent proportions of a room.
- The simplest way to mix different patterns is to combine those which share a colour in common.
- Lighting alters the appearance of texture; strong light plays it down, while shadow brings it into relief.

Left: here's a pretty mix of patterns. The floral motifs in the curtains have been copied, enlarged and stencilled on to the chest of drawers, making a charming piece of furniture out of a junk shop bargain.

Left: in this beautifully balanced room, the two patterns appear as quite independent designs. But take a closer look and see how well co-ordinated they are – both contain exactly the same colours and tones and are a good example of how to mix different patterns.

Imagine an all-white room in which every surface is smooth; the effect is hard and clinical. Now think of the same room with different textures added – a carpet with a velvety pile, a sofa covered in coarsely woven fabric and fine muslin curtains. Although all of these newly introduced materials are white, the hardness has been relieved and the room seems much more inviting.

Texture and pattern are the two final tools in the interior decorator's kit. Properly used, they are a subtle way of refining a colour scheme. Both are as evocative as colour; every texture provokes a sensation of how it feels to the touch, every pattern has a historical or cultural association.

What is meant by texture is the tactile characteristics of a material, both real and psychological – what it feels like when you touch it, and how you imagine it will feel like when you see it.

Like colours, textures can be divided into two categories, warm and cool. Warm textures – wool, brick, wood and cork, for example – have rough, non-reflective surfaces. Cool textures are the opposite – smooth, shiny and usually cold to the touch; they include stainless steel, glazed tiles, mirror, glass and gloss paint.

Left: texture and pattern play a subtle but important part in this bedroom. The grey-veined fire surround is the starting point. The striped wallpaper picks up the grey and adds pink. Grey is taken further in the blind and pillow. Textures are similar: cold marble, glossy paintwork and smooth cottons.

Below: geometric patterns are the talking point of this stylish bedroom. The amount of pattern is controlled and used sparingly to great effect. Windows are set in a navy frame with a simple red chequered edge. The dramatic introduction of striped bedlinen piped in red and matching rug are the final touches.

Without even using colour, visual interest can be created by contrasting one texture with another, as in the example above: rough against smooth, gloss paint against matt, brick against wood.

The way light falls on them affects the way the different textures show up – shadows tend to emphasize texture while direct light plays it down. Plan the lighting with texture in mind or subtle textures can be lost altogether.

Pattern has a certain sense of order about it, with its repetition of shapes – a repeated printed motif or a regular grouping of modular shapes such as a tiled floor.

It is important to consider scale carefully when choosing patterns. If you are planning to use pattern over a large surface area, such as the walls or windows, borrow a large sample before committing yourself to it. Large patterns make a room seem smaller; small designs do the opposite.

One way to mix patterns is to put together several that share the same colours. For inspiration look at how, in co-ordinated ranges of fabrics – bedlinen and so on – colours are repeated but scales are varied. You'll soon become more confident about mixing patterns, and start combining designs of contrasting colours.

s any interior designer knows, paying attention to detail is the way to achieve that very finished look, and is the sign of a professionally planned and executed scheme.

With a little care and imagination you can re-create this look in your own home – but in your own individual way. The key is to follow your instincts, rather than fads.

or use a special paint technique on a splashback.

All these decorative techniques will bring out your creative flair – but don't neglect the routine groundwork. Inadequate prepartion will make the final result look amateurish, however brilliant your ideas are. The extra effort will reward you with a really professional polish.

Below: picking out the beading in a deep peach creates a world of difference in this bedroom, making the door a focal point and breaking up the walls. To copy this, you'll need a steady hand – and masking tape.

Right: kitchen cabinets painted in pale colours are all the rage, and with good reason. They're both practical and highly stylish. One way to lift them out of the ordinary is to stencil garlands of flowers on the doors. Stencil kits are readily available in a wide choice. You can protect designs with varnish, but it may cause yellowing.

Once you have worked out what colours, textures and patterns to use, it's time to think about the finishing touches that will give your scheme finesse. Take a wardrobe that has been painted cream, for example. You could pick out the beading in navy for a crisp look, in a soft yellow for subtlety or a cheerful red, or you could decorate the door panels with a spatter effect. Brass knobs could be replaced with porcelain ones and the interior lined with pretty paper. Any piece of furniture can benefit from a little attention. Paint it, stencil it, decorate it with stripes and leopard's spots. Make it stand out or blend in, but above all don't forget it. (For decorative painting techniques, see pages 110-119.)

You can add painted murals in children's bedrooms (special kits are now available from DIY stores), a stencilled border at ceiling height in the living room,

Below centre: a black and white zebra pattern gives life to an old chair. It's easy to do, although you need a little patience. Simply paint black spots over a white background and take inspiration from abstract art.

Top right: too often, white kitchens can look clinical and rather uninviting. Here's a clever way to spice them up, using the simple but effective technique of paint-spattering over a plain surface.

Below right: a Beatrix Potter mural covers the wall in this corner of a child's attic bedroom. Complex designs are best left to those with artistic skills. Enlarge the pattern on a grid or use a mural kit, which is even easier.

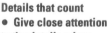

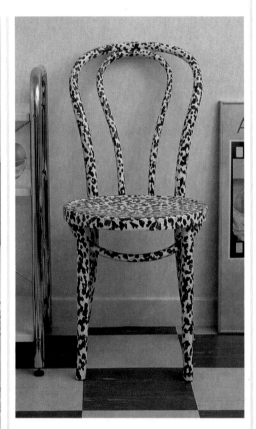

**Details that count**
● Give close attention to the details when finishing off a room scheme.
● With imagination, you can give your home a really professional designer touch.
● The smallest details count as much as the large ones do.
● Try special paint techniques, such as marbling and stencilling. They provide many ways for you to create your own individual look.
● Furniture can be decorated, and even rescued, in style. Preparation is most important when you use paint, if you want your results to look their best.

# COLOUR

## IN THE HOME

Any interior designer will tell you that most people have a good idea of the colours they like to live with. In fact, most of us have more colour experience – and expertise – than we imagine. By reading books and magazines, looking at the room sets in shop windows and visiting the homes of friends and acquaintances we can't help acquiring our own personal code of colour preference. What's sometimes difficult is knowing just how to turn this into a pleasing colour scheme. The rooms illustrated on the following pages will help show how that can be done.

Colour in the home is applied on a very large scale. It isn't in the same league as matching up clothes and accessories, or making an inspired choice of tapestry colours. Any review of colour taste in the home will reveal a strong inclination towards warm, relaxing colour schemes and a thumbs down to aggressive, strident contrasts. Though we all have favourite colours we'd like to employ, we tend to avoid – in the most used areas of the house, at least – strong or dominant colours that demand a particular style of decor. Rooms are for living in, after all, not for living up to. Youthful experiments with black rooms or aubergine-flavoured walls are seldom repeated!

Left: warm yellow amplifies the light in a south-facing room. Above: a rich wall colour will reflect a northern light handsomely.

Simple schemes, warm and easy to live with, can sometimes end up looking bland. When a room turns out that way, it is usually because colours have been matched too relentlessly with not enough variation in tone and little or no colour accent. The sitting room illustrated on the opposite page is a good example of colour used in a positive and inviting way, combining lightness and warmth with the piquancy of a very accurately judged accent colour. On the light side are the white paintwork and ceiling, a neutral carpet, an important off-white sofa, and fabric for curtains and blinds with a discreet pattern laid on a light ground. Walls are light too, but the paint colour is a lovely warm mid-yellow which reflects a golden light over the whole room. Then there's that soft jade green lifted out of the printed fabric and used to cover the two chairs. It pulls the whole room together.

The aspect of a room is important in deciding which colours to use for the decorations. Rooms facing south enjoy the sun for most of the day and the light will look warm. Pale colours, warm or cool, suit south-facing rooms in our climate – look at that sitting room opposite again. It's tailor-made for a warm aspect. Rooms that look to the north respond to warm, striking decorating colours as shown in the close-up picture on the left.

The effect of the tungsten electric light, or standard light bulb, that we switch on in the evenings is to produce a light that is close to daylight but slightly yellower. It makes red tones look richer and deeper, but tends to suppress blues and greens. So consider treating a south-facing room that's used only in the evenings with a scheme more obviously appropriate to a north-facing one.

Colour rules aren't really as rigid as they sometimes sound. If you love cool blues you can safely put them into a northerly sitting room against a background of coral or yellow. It is only when cool colours are chosen for walls or flooring, the large expanses of a room, that they seem to chill the atmosphere.

**B**eige and cream are colours which belong to the range described as neutral, but although they don't possess the intensity of pure hues, it's a mistake to regard them as either passive or even dull. As a general term, cream covers a range of tints from milky off-white to palest butter yellow; likewise beige, which can be many tones from a light greyish buff to a warm pale brown. Don't fall into the trap of treating them just as safe standby colours, when thoughtful planning can produce a subtly vibrant scheme that is easy and pleasant to live with.

Discover the underlying intonations of the neutrals which can create a distinct atmosphere while forming a clean background for various furnishing styles and colour details. Beige and brown can have a cool, slate-grey or green tinge or, at the opposite end of the spectrum, a glowing touch of red. A rich cream has a similar brilliance to sunshine yellow, but is easier on the eye and doesn't clash with existing furniture and soft furnishings. Carefully chosen with an eye to the contrast of warm and cool tones and the range of subtle colour values, the so-called neutrals can produce a vibrantly active or softly sophisticated effect.

The hallway supplies a framework for the rooms opening off it, and a harmonious scheme leads you elegantly to the different aspects of the kitchen, living room or dining areas. Its character is affected by the colour details and style of the furnishings continually glimpsed through the open doors, and sometimes it is inappropriate to pick a dominating and competing colour for the hall itself. The function, too, is important; a hall is a traffic area and the decor should not accentuate any existing feelings of clutter or gloom. Alternatively, the hallway may be so large that it seems cavernous or unfriendly, in which case you could consider turning part of it into a small study or seating area.

Pale tints and subtle colouring give a sense of openness and reflect light, encouraging easy access from room to room and on the stairs. The picture shows a unified scheme that creates a warm, luminous atmosphere. A dado rail adds horizontal emphasis in the open, well-proportioned space. Above the rail, the walls are palest cream; the dado itself has a rich tinge of yellow which enhances the textural interest of the painted embossed wallpaper. Separating these and also used for paintwork on the skirting, door and window frames and the banister rail, a gentle pale caramel accentuates distinctive lines without creating harsh breaks in the overall structure. This mixes surprisingly well with the warmer natural tone of the polished wood floor and wooden furniture.

An oriental-style rug adds pattern interest and a variety of colour accents. This restrained and harmonious background offers plenty of scope for interesting finishing touches, including the ornamental plant stand and faintly marbled texture of the window blind. The furniture has been chosen with the same unifying principle in mind as for the decoration; lightly stained natural wood and appropriate styling for the hallstands, telephone table and chairs.

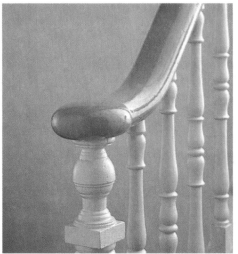

Above: the attractive detail of decoratively turned banisters is given clarity by fresh cream paint, showing the lines of the modelling through the contrast of highlight and shadow. Smooth caramel accentuates the elegant sweep and curve of the upper rail.

Above right: a dado provides a ready-made opportunity to vary wall colouring within a clearly defined area. Plain colour over an embossed surface gives intriguing detail; alternatively, a decorative paint technique would work well here.
Right: the colours of the paintwork sustain their harmony against the natural brown tones of polished wood and glossy bamboo.

Right: a welcoming atmosphere pervades the light and warmth of this colour scheme. The distinct but unobtrusive character of the hallway is echoed in all aspects of the decor and furnishings, which are in keeping with its architectural structure and its function.

# PAINT SOLUTIONS

The architectural style of a home is often most evident in the hallway. Unless there have been major structural changes, the design of the entrance and main front door, internal doors and stairwell provides the period flavour, whether traditional or modern. Inspired use of colour will help you put your individual stamp on the hallway, guided by its character and shape.

Monochromatic schemes bring unity to the different elements: in a small area a single colour scheme over walls and doors can create a stunning impact. Subtle tonal gradations and colour harmonies or even one of the special paint effects (see pages 110-119) can add interest to panelling, mouldings and alcoves without making a busy passageway look cluttered or fussy. Alternatively, plan the colour detail to provide focus, using strong hues to draw the eye to the best features and cool or neutral colours to distance or disguise the less pleasing ones. A spacious hallway with good lighting, can even take a dramatic scheme.

**Decorating Halls**
● Try to keep to one colour plan in hallways; paint doors to merge with surroundings.
● Choose a hardwearing, oil-based paint such as Dulux Satinwood.
● In well-lit hallways, try creamy mellow colours.
● Dark hallways will benefit from bold colours.
● Special paint effects can hide faults and day to day marks too, and add interest to a large wall area.

Above: the clean simplicity of a monochrome scheme in silver-grey and white accentuates details of styling and emphasizes a well-proportioned space. It creates a freshly modern atmosphere without denying the period charm of the pretty stained-glass panels, the bold black and white floor tiles and the distinctive shaping of the stair rail.

Left: this clever scheme overturns the expected colour balance. A heavy, spicy red dominates the upper walls, matched by the warm tone of stained and varnished woodwork. Surprisingly, this is offset by a pure white dado which provides a cool counterpart at low level, creating a dramatic but successful effect.

The hall, stairs and landing are the highways of the house with left turns, right turns, heavy traffic and exits. With all those doors opening into other rooms, some overall sense of colour harmony is essential in the hall area. Natural light is often poor here too – another problem to solve.

When wall surfaces are good, let paint transform the hall quickly and inexpensively. Choose a silk finish for hard wear, preferably an oil-based paint such as Dulux Satinwood for a thoroughly washable surface that provides a touch of extra light reflection too. If you are not happy with the surface, call on one of the special paint effects (described on pages 110-119) to work a subtle disguise.

If your hall is bathed in natural light, enjoy the privilege. If it has to get by on borrowed light, don't be tempted to think that lashings of pure white paint will save the day. Pale creamy tints mellow light much more comfortably. Often, though, the best strategy is to be bold. Choose a deep wall colour such as terracotta or laurel green and encourage a dark hallway to look strong and welcoming. Add good light fittings and lots of pictures, so that glass and gilt can glimmer when the lights are on.

Try to keep to one colour plan over all the wall in the area to avoid unnecessary visual breaks, and paint doors so they merge into the surrounding decorations.

Left: a stylish rug suggests an overall scheme for this modern hallway. Its geometric pattern combines creamy yellow, beige and grey touched with black, the colours of which are reworked in the decor with a subtly atmospheric effect.

Far left: a plainly styled hall becomes a work of abstract art with its bold centrepiece of a black flush door framed in yellow, a feature copied at the tiny window. Black tiling similarly frames the floor space, and cream-painted walls discreetly hold the balance.

Left: the richness of natural colour provides a cue for the interior of a country house. Gentle earth brown is the serene background chosen for the traditional style of this hallway with its polished antique mahogany and gilt-framed pictures. Pure white paintwork gives a neutral colour, but provides a refreshing tonal contrast.

n many homes that have a dining room, the chances are that it's a small area squeezed in between the kitchen and living room, or simply an extension of one or other of these spaces. In a converted flat or maisonette, it may be an awkward shape, a small area in the attic or basement that has curious niches and sloping walls. Particularly if this is your first home, you may be on a tight budget but anxious to make the most of the decor so you can create a pleasing environment for yourself and your visitors with the minimum outlay.

Paint is the least expensive and most versatile decorating material available. In a small dining area, fresh, lightweight colours are often your best option, giving an illusion of space. The yellows chosen for this small attic dining room create the cheering effect of spring sunshine whatever the weather outside. The basic colour of the ceiling and upper walls is white with a hint of primrose, deepened on the interestingly-panelled dado to an almost buttercup yellow. The primrose window frame, skirting and curtain pole provide a soft link between the two tints.

Large areas of flat, plain colour sometimes look dull or uninteresting, but in this room a carefully chosen wallpaper border breaks up the walls and draws the eye to the unusual dado. The pretty primrose flower design of this border picks up the theme colour, yellow, and adds soft sage green on a white background to the scheme. Decorating a room with paint and a paper border is less expensive than using wallpaper, with the added bonus that you don't run the risk of overwhelming a small room with too much pattern, making it seem smaller than ever, and even claustrophobic. The muslin curtains provide some privacy while maintaining the clear, fresh feel of the room. In this room, the naturally pale colour of the muslin gives the decoration an extra highlight, but of course it can easily be dyed to match the colour of walls or soft furnishings.

Left: a wooden curtain pole gets a new lease of life with a fresh coat of yellow paint. This and the matching primrose flower border soften the effect of painting the walls and ceiling in the same colour. Muslin makes inexpensive but charming curtaining.

Left: the border of pretty primroses accentuates the horizontal lines of the dado and introduces soft colours that blend in beautifully with the yellows of the woodwork and walls. The border also counteracts the effects of a very high ceiling by making the walls seem shorter than they really are. A paper border is a quick and effective way to introduce pattern to a plain wall.

Left: every detail of this room has been chosen to create a sunny, fresh, atmosphere. Even the bentwood chairs have been given pale yellow cushions. The painted panelling of the dado not only gives distinction to the lower half of the walls but also protects it from young, sticky fingers!

Left: a wide window throws a pool of clear light across this delightful attic dining room which has been specially designed to reflect the existing daylight with its own sunny colours. The result is a room of spring colours that look and feel cheerful even on the darkest of days. The deep dado has been turned into a strong feature in its own right. The two paper borders counteract the effects of a high ceiling by giving horizontal emphasis and making the walls seem shorter than they are.

Above: deep apricot walls freshened with white paintwork, ceiling and furniture relate easily to the natural wood in the room and make a sophisticated partnership with grey tablecloth and chair seats. Cool colour touches contribute to the feel. Even the picture has been chosen to fit the discipline of the scheme. Details like matching candles are planned, too.

These days, a separate dining room is quite a luxury. Though it suits most of us to take everyday meals in the kitchen if there's space, when friends come for a meal or there's a family celebration a well-laid table in a room nicely detached from kitchen clutter really sets the scene.

Dining rooms offer great scope for decoration because they are seldom everyday rooms, so different ideas about colour and style can apply. The table should be the accepted centrepiece of the room, so colour should enhance the sense of occasion and not put you off your food. Imagine the shock to the taste buds of bright raspberry walls caught in the same gaze as roast beef and gravy!

Traditionally, dining room schemes have revolved round deep opulent colours: crimson, dusky terracotta, rich green or midnight blue, and the reasoning behind this is valid. Formal meals are usually served in the evening and the combination of deep background colours and clever lighting puts the all-important table, glittering with silver and glass, into focus.

Candles can cast their romantic glow over your table setting, but keep them burning tall, above eye level, otherwise their glare will come between cross-table conversation. If a pendant light is to hand

# PAINT SOLUTIONS

Whatever the shape and location of your dining area, its decor should reflect certain priorities in your lifestyle. If you entertain formally, plan a scheme of simple elegance which is practical for daily use but can be quickly converted to create a more sophisticated atmosphere when required.

For a dining area in the kitchen, devise an informal but unusual colour scheme. Be sure to select a hardwearing paint finish such as Dulux Satinwood.

Above: pure white creates a cool, clean atmosphere for dining but it can appear rather stark when used in abundance. Here, this problem is solved by using a creamy tint with a hint of green on the walls.

Above: yellow, blue and green create a subtle harmony when the tones are perfectly balanced. Pale sea-green walls are framed by petrol blue, a colour which lends weight and density but is not too dark, while bright yellow furnishings add a high note.

over the table, make sure it is low enough to conceal the whole bulb from view.

Other light fittings in a dining room should throw their beam only where it is needed – over a serving table, for instance. The table alone needs its pool of light; the rest of the room can be left in shadow.

Deep painted walls look splendid with dark wood and antique furniture. Pick pale pinks, peach or apricot, mid-yellow too, if you are dining off a light wood or a pale glossy lacquered finish. Blue in a dining room can be fresh as gingham napkins and, like green, looks specially good with teak – often a difficult wood to integrate – and with pine.

Right: the wholesome, clean partnership of deep green and white appears in reverse here. This time walls get the light white treatment while green is used to give the paintwork interest and impact. Green frames an uncurtained window and its view of trees, and on other woodwork green gives a linear punch to the room that's echoed in an expressive choice of seating.

Basic planning makes the difference between a kitchen that's a pleasure to work in and one that's like an obstacle course. Whether you're planning a kitchen entirely from scratch, or simply modernizing or converting an existing arrangement, your main considerations should be the shape and size of the room, the way you intend to use the space and last, but not least, how colour can achieve the look you want.

An efficient kitchen layout makes use of the advantages of the overall space and minimizes the disadvantages. The important elements in the plan are the cooker and food preparation areas, sink and drainage units, worktops and storage space. Think about the logical sequence of these units. It is helpful, for example, to have a broad expanse of worktop between the cooker, sink, and refrigerator in a 'work triangle', one end for chopping and washing food, the other for the utensils and ingredients in use as you cook. Food storage should be convenient to the sink and cooker, and storage for crockery near to the serving areas. In terms of design, the kitchen space to some extent dictates the best solution to the layout. Attractive as an island unit may be, it is not a suitable fixture in a narrow kitchen, nor is a U-shaped plan helpful if you have to cross a vast space to collect a pan or plate.

These are only examples of the elements to be taken into account – specific considerations must be based on your own individual requirements. Take into account whether the kitchen is used for any extra activities such as laundry or children's hobbies or, as in a bedsit or small apartment, it's part of the living area and visible when you are reading, working or relaxing. If so, adapt the basic kitchen plan accordingly, then consider how decoration and furnishings can create the atmosphere of the room and adjust or disguise its imperfections to make the kitchen as attractive as it is functional.

Above: a small kitchen must be organized well – storage space here is compact but plentiful. To counter the boxed-in effect, bright yellow gloss against white walls creates a sunny, open atmosphere and louvred cupboard doors provide interesting texture.

Right: all the units and appliances here follow the shape of the room, emphasizing its unusual slanted corners. This stream-lined arrangement is practical and uncluttered, while the soft pink on ceiling and alcoves adds a warmth and prettiness.

The kitchen is a busy area, so plan with maximum conveniences and safety in mind. Most kitchens conform to one of the basic plans shown here: each has a logical arrangement of appliances and worktops which makes it easy to move from one area to another for efficient food preparation, cooking and washing up. Storage space should be sufficient, whether ranged around the walls at floor or eye level in the U- or L-shaped plans, or part of a neat free-standing island unit. Galley kitchens and in-line arrangements are economical of space.

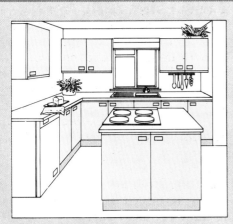

**Island kitchen:** A useful scheme to break up a large expanse of floor in a good-sized room.

**L-shaped kitchen:** Making the most of awkward space needs a careful planning sequence.

**U-shaped kitchen:** Adaptable to square or oblong rooms, giving free access to all areas.

**Galley kitchen:** Although confined, this is a highly practical use of space.

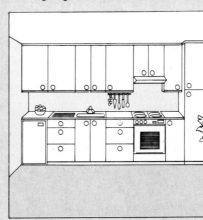

**In-line kitchen:** An ideal plan for one-room living or a narrow space conversion.

**Island**

**L-shaped**

**U-shaped**

**Galley**

**In-line**

BASIC KITCHEN PLANS

**Planning a Kitchen**
● Have a look at the basic kitchen plans and decide which is most appropriate and practical for your kitchen. List the appliances and furniture which have to be fitted in to the space.
● Make sure you have enough worktop areas and storage space to suit your needs for food preparation and cooking.
● Plan the decor with the overall design of the kitchen in mind. Remember that colour can disguise the less pleasing aspects of the room and emphasize its good points.
● If you are moving cupboards and stripping walls, make good all the surfaces before starting redecoration.

Curtain pole and timber-clad ceiling are painted creamy yellow to co-ordinate with kitchen units while fresh cotton curtains in a modern floral print combine the grey-blue of the walls with yellow and add a splash of red for contrast.

Useful objects also contribute to the scheme. All the china is blue and white, from the robust everyday tableware to the more delicate ornamental pieces. In contrast, all the fittings, including these shelves, are painted creamy yellow.

Keep to a colour theme when collecting china and you'll create an unusual display — or a unique dinner service. These plates all repeat the blue which covers the walls, as does the striped china which is easily replaced and more suitable for day-to-day use.

The country kitchen comes to town in a cream and blue setting that's brimful of natural goodness. Warm textures and natural materials are synonymous with the countryside, so wood is used extensively for the kitchen units, work top and furniture and for the timber-clad ceiling and curtain pole. All the fittings are painted a creamy yellow for co-ordination, to add warmth and reflect the maximum amount of light. Light is a necessary consideration in many country homes where small windows are a traditional feature of cottage kitchens. In contrast, the free-standing furniture is protected by clear varnish which allows the beauty of the grain to show through and safeguards it too.

The successful blend of natural and painted wood works equally well in reverse, where natural wood units contrast with brightly painted furniture. Simply remember to be consistent in your approach so that kitchen cabinets are painted in one colour and decorative pieces in another. Doors can be painted to blend or contrast with units and items you may not want to emphasize, such as window frames and skirting boards, are decorated to merge with the walls. For a subtle change of emphasis, consider using coloured varnish in place of paint for a delicate translucent effect.

Contrasting with cream is the cool blue covering the walls, a receding colour which increases the impression of space. It is repeated in the decorative plates, more appropriate in a kitchen setting than a collection of pictures, in the boldly striped china, and in the cotton curtains where it is combined with cream in a floral print.

There's nothing expensive or unusual about this kitchen. The cupboards are made from flat-pack units and the traditional furniture is still readily found — and reasonably priced. Best of all, because it doesn't rely on weathered beams or a stone floor for effect, it's a look that can be created in any home, new or old.

The 'country' kitchen has a charm and freshness all its own, but you don't have to live in a cottage or in the country to create this effect for yourself! It's a style that will suit almost any kitchen, whatever kind of home you have. Here, walls are painted grey-blue and complemented by creamy yellow on the ceiling, shelves and kitchen units for a natural, light look. To contrast, the kitchen furniture is simply varnished to enhance and protect the warm glow of wood. Bright curtains and china on display give just the right finishing touches.

The kitchen has a well-defined function, but this doesn't mean the time you spend there is solely devoted to cooking and washing up. In many homes today, the kitchen is likely to double as a dining area, for breakfast and snack lunches or suppers, if not for formal entertaining. If it is a large room, it often becomes the centre of family activities and may serve partly as a dining room, hobbies area, laundry or simply a place for relaxation. But even the smallest kitchen, which only just accommodates the cooker, sink and worktops, is a place where you may spend a surprising proportion of your time, and it is always worthwhile trying to create a pleasant and stimulating atmosphere.

If the kitchen is a light room with a good window area, its natural brightness can be emphasized with a choice of pastel or vivid paintbox colours. Pure white gives a sparkling effect of cleanness and airy spaciousness, but it needs to be kept spotless if it is

Left: a pretty, well-lit kitchen leading to a flower-filled patio is an attractive prospect, here made even more striking by the contrast of deep blue cupboards against spotless white walls. The discreetly patterned blue blind over the door is a clever finishing touch.

**Kitchen Decor**
● Plan kitchen decor to create a mood that's both pleasant and practical, and to suit the way you make use of the room.
● Use pale or bright colours to make the most of natural light.
● Disguise imperfect surfaces with deep colours or lightly textured effects.
● Emphasize an orderly sequence of kitchen units with contrasting colour.

Right: the hallway sometimes forms a useful kitchen extension (here it houses the washing machine and dryer) but such confined spaces can seem gloomy. An almost startling yellow is an excellent solution for this area, lavishly applied to every surface to give a brilliant light-reflecting sheen.

## THE RIGHT PAINT

It is in the nature of kitchens that they generate heat, moisture and, unfortunately, a certain amount of grease and grime. Paintwork here must stand up to condensation and changes of temperature without cracking or peeling, or losing any attractiveness in colour and surface texture. You should be able to wash and wipe it as often as is necessary without doing any damage.

Oil-based paints are designed to withstand this sort of treatment; silk finish or matt emulsions will soon show signs of wear and tear. Satinwood paint is an ideal choice for the kitchen, giving a smooth, resistant and durable finish for walls, ceiling and woodwork. Alternatively, you can use gloss paint for any or all of these surfaces, but remember that it dries with a highly reflective shine which may be distracting in an area already cluttered with glistening utensils. However, gloss to sustain its original impact. White walls make a good background for a strong, clear colour in other paintwork – the primary colours yellow, red and blue always look fresh and lively, while dark tones set against white can be most striking.

Monochromatic schemes (using a single colour or tones of one colour) can appear cool and reserved or dramatic and intense. Yellow and orange are sunny colours which can cheer up the day to day chores. In a small room, strong or deep hues can be used to give a distinctive identity which might be overwhelming in a larger space.

Certain paint techniques can disguise a less than perfect wall surface. Heavy textures are inappropriate as they are hard to keep clean, but a subtle sponged or ragged texture (see pages 112-115) can make effective cover for a slightly uneven wall. Tones of one colour applied in soft layers or a close harmony of mingled colours provide a special touch that gives the kitchen individuality and charm.

Left: blue offers a wide range of tones that make attractive decorating possibilities. This kitchen gains a fresh, light effect from a clear, unusual pastel blue tint. Some thought has been given to pointing up a warmer tone in the furnishings and accessories, where pink and pale apricot complement the cooler combination of blue and white.

can give an effective lift to a kitchen scheme when restricted to limited areas. You could, for example, follow the traditional use of gloss over door and window frames, cupboard fronts and shelving. Satinwood gives a softer sheen than gloss but an equally tough finish.

There's another problem to solve if your kitchen has laminated panels or worktops which need rejuvenating. It is possible to paint over a laminate with slightly diluted gloss paint, but this is inadvisable as the surface inevitably chips with time and the result can soon become tatty and unhygienic. It is better to remove the offending surfaces altogether and substitute fresh materials. If you don't particularly need to replace a laminated surface and you have a solid wood base underneath, you can strip the laminate right back and prepare the wood for painting to match the rest of the decor.

# PAINT SOLUTIONS

**T**he Satinwood range of paints is an ideal choice in the kitchen, with an excellent colour range on offer to help you create the background atmosphere you want. Before you embark on any scheme, however, remember that efficiency and safety are most important in the kitchen, and the way it is decorated can

opportunities for decorative colour variation. If you favour a monochromatic, or single colour, scheme, a recess can be emphasized with a slightly darker shade of the chosen colour, or visually 'lit' with a noticeably paler tint. Alternatively, a contrast colour can look equally effective – even strong colour combinations work well

Left: a compact sink unit fits neatly into the angle below a slanted ceiling and benefits from the spacious impression created by cool blue-grey paintwork. The colour has a subtle, subdued appeal that's brightened by the strong red of the door handles and kitchen accessories.

assist these factors – as well as being a pleasing element of the design. Good lighting is vital in an area where knives and pans of hot liquid are commonly in use; the colour scheme should not interfere with available light or cast baffling reflections in any already cramped areas. Plain colour acts as a neutral backdrop for a busy situation; site high gloss surfaces or special paint effects with care so that they display their own qualities to advantage without competing with the functional aspects.

Kitchens often have small recesses and alcoves – these can provide discreet

if they are carefully balanced.

Many other details in the kitchen will provide scope to introduce attractive colour touches. Shelving, hanging racks, drawer and cupboard handles can be picked out in fresh, bright colours. If mundane objects such as water pipes and ventilators must be visible, why not make a

Above: all-over colour gives a lively feel. Here a refreshing mix of two sunshine yellow hues is highlighted by the crisp white lines of window and door frames.

feature of them by painting them in bold contrast? Of, if you prefer, hide or blend them with the colour of the walls using Satinwood.

More than anywhere else in the home, the kitchen takes much of its overall look from the objects in it. You may have a favourite set of plates which are kept on

**Decorating Kitchens**
● Use a colour scheme to enhance and clarify the functional aspects of the kitchen design.
● Don't use dark colours in areas that are already shadowed, or highly reflective paint surfaces in cluttered spaces.
● Disguise unsightly pipes and projections by painting them in the same colour as the walls. If you prefer to make a feature of them, use a brightly contrasting colour.
● Take a colour cue from existing objects when planning a face-lift for the kitchen; patterned china, plants or curtain fabric could inspire you.

display; patterns on china are often a source of delightful colour combinations to copy. The bright colours of plastic kitchenware also suggest bold possibilities for the decor: plain walls, for example, could benefit from a pretty stencilled border (see pages 116-117) which picks up and echoes these vivid tones.

Left: primary colours aren't just for children – they can add a vivid sense of fun to a small kitchen and brighten the domestic chores. The curious niches and angles of this little room are boldly picked out in red, yellow and blue against a clean white background. Pot plants are a pleasing and inexpensive way to add an extra dash of colour.

Left: this galley kitchen features an economical arrangement of fittings to make the most of the narrow area. Strong colour emphasizes the well-ordered impression and the lighter toned lining of the panelled doors avoids a monotonous effect.

hen is a kitchen not a kitchen? When it's a kitchen/dining room – but although it's convenient to eat in the room where food is prepared, a kitchen/dining room needs careful planning to be a success.

First consider what sort of room it is to be. Do you want a breakfast bar to cater for snacks? A farmhouse kitchen with a scrubbed table at which you can prepare food and serve your family with leisurely meals? Or would you prefer an open-plan arrangement which has a kitchen plus dining room *en suite*? Whichever you choose, the dining space should co-ordinate with the kitchen to form an integrated room, though it's often a good idea to define the dining area with subtle lighting or painted stencils. Unless your kitchen is particularly large, the most difficult problem will be how to accommodate the table. For tiny kitchens look for ranges of units featuring tables or breakfast bars designed to complement the cupboards, or choose gateleg or narrow pine tables for a country scheme. Medium-sized kitchens can take a round table which provides a welcome contrast to the oblong cabinets, while a long refectory, trestle, or traditional kitchen table can be placed in the middle of a large kitchen. Unless your room is very big, put the table to one side, away from the work triangle of the cooker, sink and fridge — but remember to allow sufficient room for the diners to get in and out! Above all, consider the colour scheme. While a working kitchen can be bright and cheery or cool and clinical, a kitchen/dining room needs to be an attractive place in which to eat as well as cook.

Left: pale pink defined by burgundy is the perfect, if surprising, choice for this kitchen/dining room, adding warmth, light and prettiness to walls, blind and units at minimal cost.

Left: compensate for a lack of architectural features by creating your own stencilled border. This rose design in three colours adds burgundy and green to the prevailing pink for emphasis and provides an attractive garland above the door and window frames.

Left: DIY kitchen units are transformed by this simple dragged finish. The arch is outlined in burgundy and white to give distinction to the doors and the frame is painted white for freshness. Co-ordinating door knobs add simple style.

Left: second-hand chairs are painted white and decorated with the rose motif which adorns the walls to give originality and style — and all for the price of a pot of paint! Cotton fabric disguises a chipboard table and forms an inexpensive window covering.

iving rooms often receive the most attention with regard to decor, because they are the focal points and showpieces of the home. Here, it's appropriate to create an atmosphere which is attractive and comfortable, inviting to both the occupants and guests.

Elsewhere in the house, decorative treatments often have to take their cue from necessary fixtures and fittings, such as in the kitchen and bathroom. In the living room, however, your scheme can allow a freer rein to such considerations as atmosphere, shape and colour. The extent of your scope here depends on the available space, existing furniture and fittings and on whether the room has to incorporate areas for play and study. Schemes may have to be practical to withstand everyday use by children and pets as well as providing relaxing surroundings for after-dinner conversation.

Colour and light are the important factors in setting – and changing – the mood of your living room. Lighting is the key to the room's different aspects by day and by night. When choosing colours, you should take into account the type of light which enters the room by day – is it a cool north light or strong sunlight; a neutral, even light by day or glowing rays in late afternoon. In the evening, do you prefer strong lighting from a central source, or the soft glow of several lamps discreetly placed around the room? Colour can be used to pick up and play upon the natural atmosphere of the room, or adjust and counter its less appealing aspects.

Cool colour schemes lend sophistication to a large room and give the appearance of more space in a small area. Subtle tints form a clean background for the distinctive lines of modern furniture, for pictures, ornaments and shelving displays. Clever lighting can warm up colour by night and play on its reflective qualities, varying the apparent scale and perspective of the room, while shadows can be used to create brilliant focal points of illumination and veil the surrounding space.

Above: sky blue is a vibrant yet light colour, teamed freshly here with white. The smooth sheen of paintwork and soft furnishing materials respond to the light, set off by touches of warm, bright colour.

**Living Room Decor**
- Use colour to create mood in the room and plan lighting to alter its character by day and night.
- Offset a cool colour scheme with touches of warmer hues; contrast bright against subdued colours to avoid monotony.
- Employ texture as a design feature – silk or matt finish for walls, gloss for woodwork, matt and shiny fabrics on soft furnishings.
- Plan a colour scheme which is practical for everyday use of the room by adults and children.

Left: the colour scheme of this room has an understated brilliance which creates an air of elegance. With its cool manner and subtle tints, the furnishing style demonstrates a clever marriage of comfort and sophistication, making the most of the open, well-proportioned space.

Left: the window area is the most striking feature of this room, filtering bright, cool light across the broad space. The design of the room is spare and uncluttered; clean white paintwork emphasizes the natural light. The warm earthy browns and dense blue-greys in the furnishings are melodious partners.

# LIGHT FITTINGS

downlighter

pendant light

spotlight

wall light

wall light

standard uplighter

angled uplighter

table lamps

Light fittings have a practical purpose but they also contribute to style and atmosphere in a room. They should be carefully planned in conjunction with the overall scheme.

The ceiling-mounted pendant is the traditional single source of central lighting. Modern pendant fittings can be raised or lowered to cast light overall or in a focused pool. Downlights recessed in the ceiling act in the same way, but from a fixed position, while track-mounted spotlights offer powerful directional beams. Wall-mounted uplights reflect from walls and ceiling. A standard uplighter provides a movable source of light above eye level.

Many people prefer the soft glow of lamps in the living room at night, carefully placed for reading or sewing, for example, or to create a pool of light at low level. Designs for table lamps come in all shapes and sizes, casting light downwards from a traditional lampshade, upwards from a stylish cylindrical uplighter fitting.

Right: little touches add impact and style. Contrasting bands of russet and white are used to define the cornice and doorway, while the two colours merge in the decorative paint treatment used for the walls, with brown sponged over white.

Right: the varied shades of autumn combine to create a room that's warm and intimate. Nature is a continual source of inspiration for colour schemes, as this arrangement of bright chrysanthemums emphasized by a few sprays of white gypsophila shows.

Right: patterns and colours which blend soften the impact of dark colours, reducing their 'advancing' effect so that they do not encroach on space. In contrast to the usual combination of pale walls and dark carpet, this room relies on deep walls for warmth and pale flooring to reflect light.

**B**reak with convention and choose rich, dark walls and a pale carpet for a living room that always feels warm and inviting. Extra depth is added by the broken colour, which creates a sense of luxury in the living room while plain emulsion in the same base colour subtly alters the mood in the adjoining dining room. Both rooms are designed to co-ordinate, using the same paint and carpet, with furniture in similar shades and styles. Light wood and natural cane contrast with the russet walls while the simple shapes of the tables and cupboards offset the more elaborate Chesterfield and chairs. It's all a question of balance, blending traditional with new and dark with pale. A paisley pattern which continues the colour of the walls has been chosen for the curtains and upholstery, making the floor the main area of contrast. The arrangement of the furniture is important too. Note how the doorway creates a frame for the centrally placed dining table and how the living room seating is grouped to form a natural conversation piece. The writing table fits neatly against the window wall but the route to the dining table is sensibly kept clear. Light touches include the broad pale grey band defining the doorway, lamps and picture mounts — small in themselves but providing just the right degree of contrast to add freshness to this scheme.

Left: peach meets brown in a setting where rich nutmeg colours the walls and textiles to give a feeling of warmth and luxury. Sponged colour on the living room walls creates a restful atmosphere while plain emulsion makes the dining room look smart. A paler version of the dominant colour is used on the ceiling for complete co-ordination.

An open fireplace, moulded dado, chintz curtains and upholstery — all the ingredients of a traditional look that has a timeless elegance which never goes out of style. Though the days are gone of enormous houses with luxurious sitting rooms, you can still create a similar effect in your own living room, whatever its scale and architectural style.

Ragging (page 114) is a versatile technique which gives a sophisticated and antique finish. Textured walls lend character to a room, and the effects of ragging are virtually endless, according to the colours you choose for the base and top coats. Soft

Right: cool, dusky pink ragged over pinky white forms a soft background for pretty flower vases and old-style furnishings. Under afternoon light or the glow of lamps in the evening, the pink walls become mellow and warm.

Right: the wood-framed fireplace gives this room an elegant focal point, belying the fact that it was bought ready-made for easy fitting. The fireplace surround frames flat plywood panels, which have been hand-marbled, to blend in with the traditional atmosphere of the room.

tones have been chosen for this living room and the adjoining hallway, with a dusky pink over white with a hint of pink for the main room and beige for the hall.

If you live in a modern house or apartment without such details as fireplace, panelling and decorative mouldings, don't despair – you can create these features quite cheaply, and in the style you want. These sheets of plywood lined with narrow wooden beading or moulding have been transformed into panelling that instantly suggests an atmosphere of traditional comfort. The panels within the fireplace surround are finished with delicately painted marbling, an effective but less expensive finish than tiling.

The chintzes used for the curtains, loose covers and upholstery combine the right visual note with practical hardwearing qualities. Don't forget the value of well-chosen accessories in setting the scene: an antique wall-clock, elegantly framed prints and paintings and displays of fresh or dried flowers all create the right atmosphere, and a handsomely patterned rug brings a touch of class to inexpensive plain carpeting.

Above: modern rooms can sometimes seem rather stark and basic. Here, a little ingenuity, imagination and inexpensive decorating techniques have converted a plain room into something much more opulent. False panelling was fixed around the lower walls and the ready-made fireplace was easily installed. Cleverly combined paint textures and carefully chosen colours complete the country house effect.

Above: the traditional accent is continued in the hall, where the walls are rag-rolled in warm beige tones for extra emphasis. The soft sheen of the Dulux Satinwood paintwork flatters the lines of the panelled door.

# PAINT SOLUTIONS

**Decorating Living Rooms**
● The living room has a dual role as public and private space.

● **Plan colours which suit its various uses and also complement your furnishings.**
● **Make the decor**

practical, but also capable of responding to a more formal and elegant atmosphere for entertaining.

Above: a dado rail creates horizontal emphasis, providing a neat visual break that invites you to exploit colour contrast. Here, fresh buttermilk is set against slatey blue-green tones.

The living room should be one of the most versatile rooms in your home, capable of performing many functions. As well as being the place in which you can relax in privacy or entertain visitors, it may also be used as anything from a playschool to a committee room. The scheme forming the backcloth for all this activity should be as adaptable as possible, practical, and, of course, positively pleasing.

Pale colours set off both traditional and modern styles of furniture, and give the room a bright, inviting atmosphere. Pure white has long been a popular choice for its neutral qualities, but it can also be rather cold; neutral beige and grey are also popular, and rightly so, but they may have

a somewhat deadening effect in the wrong setting. A rich cream or one of the delicately tinted whites — with just a hint of pink, yellow, green or blue — won't quarrel with other aspects of the decorating scheme, but has a stimulating effect that brings the room to life. From this, you might move on to consider the still subtle but more distinctive pastels, such as buttermilk or sand, peach, apricot or pink, which provide both warmth and light.

colour scheme around existing furnishings. A plain colour can be matched with the simple harmony of a lighter or darker tone, or a mixed hue such as blue-green can offset a true blue. An opposing colour inevitably creates a more dramatic effect. Patterned furnishing fabrics offer intriguing colour cues; your paint scheme may echo the dominant hue or pick up one of the minor colour accents.

Colour can supply an illusion of spaciousness, though clever decor won't compensate for a lack of organization. Pure white walls open out the room and cool colours — silver-grey, pastel blue or delicate green — lend distance. Stronger colour accents can be added in furnishings and accessories.

Whether you are decorating a new living room or giving a facelift to familiar surroundings, you may have to plan the

Above: glowing peach paintwork is precisely balanced by the cool clarity of pale blue-grey furnishings. These complementary colours heighten and give brilliance to each other, with white making its mark as an accent colour against such distinct tints.

Above: monochromatic schemes based on warmly tinted white are softly reflective and always easy on the eye. In this country cottage, a single tint is taken over every painted surface to give an undisturbed visual harmony.

Below: grey used tone on tone gives this bedroom brooding presence. Furniture is palely tinted, while mid-grey carpet leads the eye to storm-grey walls. Geometric bed-linen brings all the greys into one pattern context. Accents are strong; black chair, television and lamps balance white in the picture mounts.

Decorate a bedroom with colours to rest by. Soporific shades and calm blends most suit the room's early morning/late night lifestyle. Gentle colours soothe us to sleep and don't intrude on our discomfort if we take to our beds with flu.

Colour themes that most often work for bedrooms are usually the simplest ones. Schemes based around one of the pastel colours – especially cream – touched with a single warm accent such as pink or yellow, are fail-safe. In older, dimly-lit rooms,

rich, muted colours are comforting; plain painted walls with, for example, faded chintz and oriental-type rugs are a recipe for mellow timelessness.

Busy patterns on bedroom walls and florid, strikingly patterned curtains or blinds can disturb repose by getting on your nerves as you lie in bed looking at them. Though bright colours are often employed – and enjoyed – in children's bedrooms, they run counter to the needs of most adult bedrooms and could easily be regretted first thing in the morning!

Above: pink is a soft warm colour, but used over broad expanses it can have a rather claustrophobic effect. Here, the walls have been painted in the very palest tint, with a deeper pink stripe to emphasize the lines of the room. An even more vivid colour has been chosen for the furniture and accessories.

**Decorating Bedrooms**
● Try schemes based around one colour; the natural whites or pastels are ideal for the bedroom,

particularly if it is small and dark.
● An awkwardly shaped bedroom, such as an attic room with sloping ceiling and

window, will also benefit from the use of a single colour scheme; it will help to unify all the features.
● Soft pinks and

yellows will give a warm accent to rooms that seem chilly. In dimly-lit rooms, rich, muted colours give a mellow touch.

# PAINT SOLUTIONS

Bottom: in a room shaped like this, a simple colour scheme is the best. Apricot white shows off this room's charm.

Below: children enjoy bright colours, but in a small room a bold colour scheme must be carefully planned. Cornflower blue is a clever choice, being both vivid and gentle: its clean tone is enhanced by fresh white and lively touches of primary yellow and red.

In many modern homes, only the master bedroom is of good size and proportion. Often, other small bedrooms are converted from one large room by partition walls, or tucked into an attic or extension. This means you may be confronted by a cramped, irregularly shaped or poorly lit space.

These small rooms are usually allocated to the children in a family home, and their size can be turned to advantage if you wish to redecorate frequently over the years, according to the changing needs of the growing child. No matter what their age, children often have quite definite ideas

about what they like and how they want to use their bedrooms, so try to incorporate their ideas in your plans.

Awkward spaces, such as attic rooms with sloping walls or ceilings, or partitioned rooms with cut-off corners, do not need further complication or fuss from a busy or strident colour scheme. A single colour or range of subtly graduated tones may prove the best choice, and you can pick out strong colour accents in the soft furnishings and accessories. Pale, warm tints reflect all the available light and glow softly by day or night, creating a cosy, relaxed atmosphere.

Green is regarded as a restful colour and the pale tints used in this colonial-style bedroom create a calm, cool atmosphere which offsets the warm tones of natural wood furniture and subtle apricot bedlinen. Attractively stencilled patterns add a touch of detail that's welcome in a spacious room with a broad expanse of wall.

The atmosphere of a room is largely what you make it, but its own shape and architectural detail can be suggestive of an overall scheme. This bedroom is of generous dimensions and the attractive louvred doors and window shutters have a slightly colonial air reminiscent of warm summer nights.

To complement these qualities, the decoration provides a cool elegance. This is given a delicate personal touch with pretty stencilled patterns on the walls. A background of creamy white with a hint of green sets off the subtle green tint applied to the door and window frame. Although a subdued colour, it is given faint brilliance by the paleness of the tints that have been selected. The simple charm of the stencilled motifs emphasizes the shape and structure of the room without disturbing its harmonious atmosphere. A view of the adjoining bathroom shows how the overall scheme of the bedroom is echoed there with a slightly warmer tint of peach.

The carefully selected furnishings are comfortably appropriate in this setting. Period pieces in stained and varnished wood are matched by delightful old prints in heavy frames and art nouveau lamps.

Above left: the tonal balance of the decoration is carefully preserved in the stencilled detail. A delicate tracery pattern running below the cornice provides a heavier tint of green, but is touched with white and discreetly offset by creamy yellow flowerbuds.
Left: the same scheme is used in a slightly more elaborate pattern to decorate the wooden blanket box.

Above: stencilling is an excellent edging device, used here to focus attention on an elegant wood-framed mirror. The stencil pattern repeats the discreet green used in the bedroom, now applied to a toning apricot background with a hint of warmth.

### Toddler

- Washable walls are essential for the under-fives.
- Add pattern with stencils painted on the walls and cot.
- Buy full-size furniture that's designed to last. Economize by buying short-life items (like the cot) second-hand.
- Provide flooring that's easy to clean.

### 3-12 years

- Use bright colours to create a lively atmosphere.
- Remember bunks give you two beds for the space of one.
- Provide plenty of storage for toys plus shelves for books and treasures.
- Homework begins. Make room for it!

### Teenager

- Give the room a grown-up image and let teenagers choose colour schemes.
- Allow numerous electric points for computers and hi-fi.
- Provide for friends with seating or an extra bed.
- Make the room self-contained, like a bedsit, to encourage independence.

How can you persuade your baby to go to sleep, your seven-year-old to desert the tv or your teenager to vacate the living room? The answer is to give them a room of their own that's not so much a bedroom but more a nursery/playroom/bedsitting room. It needn't be expensive. These settings show how one room can adapt to the needs of a toddler, child and teenager by a simple change of colour scheme. Look at the first room where three pieces of economical, system-built furniture, basket storage, a second-hand cot and a rocking chair provide all the furniture a pre-school child (and his mum) require. Pastel blue walls are decorated with stencils which are repeated on the cot. Chest and cupboard are joined by a worktop, used for nappy changing, and the floor is covered by sealed cork tiles which form a warm and water-resistant play surface.

Cut to age seven. 'Rupert' has graduated to bunks which cater for friends who come to tea and stay until breakfast. The room is now decorated in primary colours with yellow walls, red bunks and a blue chair in place of nursery furnishings. Otherwise, all that's changed are the unit handles, the frame of the basket storage painted red to match the bunks, and the rug.

Eight years later the bunks separate into single beds for extra lounging space and red now forms an effective contrast to a cool grey that's more in keeping with a sophisticated adolescent image. The worktop comes into its own as a desk, and there's a carpet on the floor, but, once again, this is a transformation made primarily with paint. Follow the same pattern for a daughter, varying the colours and designs. Every baby needs a cot, every child has toys, and almost every teenager has a hi-fi and homework. Build the room around their individual needs, think long term, and change colour, which is cheap, rather than furniture, which isn't. The children may be heard and not seen – but that's the price of success.

Nurseries needn't be too babyish. None of the furnishings in this room limits its use to the first years of life. The only short-term items are the cot and nursing chair, both second-hand and painted white, the rug and the painted frieze which adds interest to the pale blue walls. Balloon and teddy motifs taken from this enliven the corner, the cot and also decorate a plain roller blind for complete co-ordination.

Brighten up a bargain buy with stencils cut to repeat the pattern of a nursery frieze. This device helps co-ordinate disparate pieces of furniture.

The frieze creates a dado effect, dividing the wall and altering the room's proportions to suit a child's eye view in the early stages.

The balloons above the frieze are enlarged to make a focal point of the corner and are repeated on the stencilled second-hand cot.

Here's a room for a boy who's bound to make his name, which is stencilled on the newly-painted walls. Primary colours are used to create a welcoming room where there's plenty of space for play. The cork floor has been retained because it's the perfect surface for toy cars while the worktop, no longer needed for nappy changing, becomes a computer desk.

Below: blue, red and yellow make a scheme to suit any child. Shelves painted to contrast with the walls hold treasures which increase in number with the years.

Put your child among the stars and personalize his or her bedroom by stencilling the letters of their name on the wall in colours of your choice.

Pale grey sets the style in this teenage room, on walls which are spattered with red and blue to link with existing furnishings. The bunks have been separated to serve as day beds as well as the conventional kind and the floor now has a grey carpet to tone with the walls. The nappy changing surface is still going strong as a desk and the storage is given a third set of handles to tie it in with this soft, new scheme.

Anyone for tennis? The initial purchase of a full-size wardrobe now pays off: new handles are all that are needed for this new scheme.

Spattered walls, brightly painted skirting and co-ordinating bedlinen give a primary coloured scheme added sophistication.

The scarlet desk lamp looks as good as ever in its new setting, angled over the pillow to cater for bedside reading.

The space allotted to the bathroom in modern homes can vary from a broad, inviting area rivalling the main bedroom, to a tiny cupboard-like room with barely enough space for the necessary fittings. The functional aspect of the bathroom often takes precedence over its decorative potential. This is a pity because careful attention to colour and design can transform the meanest space into an area of distinctive character or create an atmosphere of real luxury in a generously proportioned room.

The role played by the bathroom is a key to the style to aim for. If it is a busy traffic area for a large family it will attract all sorts of clutter so the decor should be unfussy, practical and easy to clean. Alternatively, the bathroom may be a private space for leisurely relaxation; it can double as a dressing room, reading room or even a small study, as long as there is space to keep clothes, magazines, books or papers clear of the actual washing area. It can be a

Below: this airy bathroom deserves its fresh, clean colour scheme. The principle of colour contrast is cleverly applied here – pale apple green is teamed with warm pinks and apricots to good effect.

Above: pale colours emphasize this large, open space in a most successful combination of white, cream and pink offset by rich red brown in the door surround and in the Venetian blind. The slatted blind cleverly echoes the vertically arranged panelling around the bath and lower wall. Carefully selected furnishings in this bathroom create a feel which is both stylish and functional, blending modern design with a charming period air.

**Bathroom Decor**
- Treat the bathroom as an active space in design terms, not just as a service area.
- Make use of colour to enhance the room's best features and conceal imperfections.
- Use warm reds, pinks and browns to make a welcoming effect in a chilly bathroom; cool blues and greens to open out a luxurious space.
- Add interest with colour detail, such as a stencilled pattern or a narrow wallpaper border around the top of a plain wall.
- Plan accessories and ornaments to heighten the effect – brightly coloured towels and curtains, cosmetic jars, plants and pictures.

place purely for pampering yourself, full of softness and fragrance, with a large easy chair or window seat and a dressing table full of cosmetics; or a stylish but service-able washroom designed for speed and comfort. The decor in all cases can be as attractive as it is practical.

Colour is the most powerful element for changing the face of your bathroom. If the bathroom is very small, pale colours will seem to open it out, but you can make a virtue of its enclosed character by using a rich, dark, warm colour – deep red or violet, for example – to exaggerate the effect of a cosy, private haven. Another advantage of a small bathroom is that redecorating can be done relatively quickly and inexpensively, so this might be the place to try out a decorative paint tech-

nique such as stencilling (see page 116) or striping (see page 103) which will give the room individual style.

As with other rooms, you can emphasize or disguise the existing character of a bathroom. If it is a sunny room, you can afford to use cool blues, greens and greys without creating a chilly atmosphere, but warm pinks, peaches and apricots are a good choice as they reflect natural light beautifully. A bathroom with cold light may need to be given a cosier feeling with dark tones – white can create too clinical an effect – and it could also be brightened up with touches of vivid colour in accessories and details. Comfortable carpeting on the floor and a selection of thick, richly coloured towels put the finishing touches to a well-chosen scheme.

Above: a bathroom with a welcoming, lived-in look, every element suggesting that the room is a personal retreat for private relaxation. Soft grey tones enlivened by touches of colour provide a suitable background for the unusual wood-panelled bath surround which turns the bath into a substantial piece of furniture.

# PAINT SOLUTIONS

Right: relatively simple solutions are often the most elegant. Here, white and blue-grey team with natural wood and framed prints to create classic styling.

**Decorating Bathrooms**
● Use a resilient oil-based paint such as Satinwood which withstands condensation and temperature changes.
● Plan paintwork either to disguise or deliberately make a feature of visible parts of the plumbing.
● Prepare walls and surfaces adequately before painting.
● Convert awkward gaps into useful storage space and brighten them with colour detail.

The bathroom is a hardworking area, but this doesn't mean it can't be as elegant, pretty, striking or fun as any other room in the house. When it comes to decorating here it's important to choose the right materials for the job. Matt vinyl and silk finish emulsions cannot stand up to the steamy atmosphere and condensation in a bathroom, but Dulux Satinwood paint has been specially developed to cope with this problem – it's the ideal choice to keep the bathroom decor fresh and clean.

Satinwood is an oil-based paint, more resilient in damp conditions than water-based emulsions. It can therefore be used on the walls, as well as on wood and metal such as pipes and radiators. Gloss paint is only suitable for wooden panelling, wood trims and metal surfaces in the bathroom, not for walls.

Above: pure white shows the fresh, clean lines of this well-arranged, spacious bathroom. Its silvery quality is enhanced by the narrow stripes of pink and grey applied to the angles at wall and ceiling and the edges of the shelving.

Left: taking its cue from the vibrant colours of the smartly checked wallpaper, the paintwork of this neat washroom/toilet adds the finishing touch with a bold flourish.

No paint wears well unless it is applied to a well-prepared surface, so get the basics in order before moving to the final scheme. Decide whether to box in unsightly pieces of plumbing and any small spaces between bathroom fittings which will only collect dust. It may be possible to convert quite small gaps into useful extra storage space which can be attractively decorated to hold soaps, hand towels, shampoo bottles and so on. If you can't box off large pipes, paint them the same colour as the walls to disguise them, or make a virtue of necessity and feature them in a bold contrast colour. Check tiling for cracks and chips likely to deteriorate. A smooth, tough paint surface is a practical alternative to tiling.

When choosing paint colours, remember that pale tints, especially those with a glossy finish, can show up flaws on the surface of walls and ceiling, while a darker colour will tend to disguise them. Chilly bathrooms need a warm tone overall to create a cosier atmosphere, so choose colours in the red, pink, violet, brown, orange and orange-yellow range. Blues and greens tend to be cooler, but a rich ultramarine or olive green seems to shrink the proportions of the room and create an intimate feel. For maximum light, pure white has a classic appeal, but it needs some touches of colour to avoid making the room appear clinical and anonymous.

Decorative paint techniques are excellent for enlivening bathroom walls, particularly if you want to camouflage awkward irregularities: sponging, ragging and colour washing are good for all-over patterns, while stencilling can be applied more selectively to borders, panels and bathroom units (see pages 112-119).

Above: what better scheme for a large, sunny bathroom than sunshine yellow on bright white? Wood panelling painted with Satinwood or gloss is a solution as practical as it is attractive.

onservatories are really high class greenhouses – the only difference is that people share the space with the plants. The main focus of decoration here is the plants themselves – spilling from pots and urns, displayed on top of pedestals, climbing up trelliswork and trailing from hanging baskets – and they'll provide the dominant colour in any scheme.

The traditional conservatory should ideally be painted white to show off its handsome structure. Green paint is the only really feasible alternative to white, though it may subdue the impact of both plants and architecture.

A modern one-off conservatory could use a more adventurous colour range, though you might prefer to make a feature of the hardwood structure itself. Wood, like most natural materials, provides a complementary background for plants.

Conservatory floors are often tiled, but a sheet vinyl flooring is a good alternative. Quarry tiles were the Victorian and Edwardian choice, sometimes laid in complex tessellated patterns but often in a simple check of red and black. Glazed ceramic tiles can look wonderfully exotic while glazed terracotta exudes rustic charm. Whatever flooring you propose to use, it must be able to take the inevitable spillage while watering all those plants!

A glass conservatory on the south side of the house will become unbearably hot in summer and blinds may be an essential accessory. Most conservatory manufacturers can fit blinds of either the Venetian type or those made from fabric backed with reflective metal foil. For fabric blinds, plain parchment is a classic choice or, if you prefer a pattern, choose stripes.

## GARDEN FURNITURE

ind a sheltered corner of the garden for table and chairs to summer outside. Painted in gloss or treated with Dulux Woodsheen, they won't need bringing indoors every time it rains. Weatherproof materials for furniture include rotproof moulded resin and solid teak. Oil teak occasionally to preserve its colour or simply let it fade to a pleasing silvery grey. Cast iron is decorative and traditional, though cast aluminium copies are much lighter to move around. Cane and rattan are perfect for the conservatory, and, if well painted, they too can stay outside come rain or shine.

Left: any south-facing room with generous windows can be given the conservatory feel. This spacious-looking arrangement is achieved by hanging some plants from above and using tall mirrored planters as well as low level pots for ferns.

Far left and below: two attractive, spacious conservatories recently built in traditional style display a blend of classic materials, lush plants and coolly tiled floors. Cast iron and painted willow provide the furniture.

The outside of a house is its public face. We share it not only with our neighbours but with passers-by who will – we hope – like what they see. We owe a duty to them all.

It is not only the important listed building that needs to be cherished; all old buildings and many of this century, are recognized as having a welcome individuality of character and detailing. To remove or change the distinguishing features of a house by putting unsympathetic modern windows in a period façade, for instance, or by adding a Tudor-style door to a nineteenth century cottage, can actually downgrade the value of the property. To change is not always to improve.

Although exterior decorations are cosmetic, it is vital to get them right because the time and cost involved in doing the job is so high. One way to tackle the decision making is to take a black and white photograph of the house straight on and have it slightly enlarged. Make a series of tracings from the photograph and then use felt-tipped pens to experiment with colour blends. Take your efforts outside to compare them with the actual house in its surroundings, and then see how you feel about it.

If your house is in the country, the landscape and local architectural traditions will guide your choice of exterior decoration. In town streets, your colour scheme will be part of the communal canvas. If it is one of a row or terrace, it makes sense to decorate in line with the prevailing style. To paint over the facade of a house in a brick-built terrace so that visually it jumps out of the row could have neighbours up in arms and with justification.

## PAINTED DOORS

Left: harmonious individuality expressed in a row of terraced town cottages with colourwashed façades. Each house makes its single statement yet the group remains easy on the eye. The soft colours plus white in the Dulux Weathershield Masonry paint range will give any row of houses a similar well composed outlook.

Right: timber-framed weatherboarded house, typical of some areas of the south-east of England, particularly Essex and Kent, dates from the eighteenth century. Here it's been given the classic treatment: white paint outlined in black is crisp and fresh against the strong greens and reds of the flower garden.

**Exterior Decoration**
- Choose colour schemes that work with the surroundings; in the country, the landscape and local architecture will guide you; in towns, choose style and paint to blend in with the rest of the row.
- Modern houses can take bolder colour schemes, but avoid garish colours on older houses.
- Take into consideration any period details when decorating an old house, and try to enhance them.
- The Dulux Matchmaker Masonry paint range is devised to co-ordinate with regional stone variations and there are over 40 colours to choose from.

ooking from left to right, subdued grey brickwork tinged with pink is perfectly teamed with dark green paintwork – an appealing echo of the glossy sheen of overhanging foliage. Next, a pink highlight is used to pick out the plasterwork – an individuual touch on this terraced house. This bright yellow half-glazed door in the third picture beckons a sunny welcome into the house by extending the colour theme to the hall beyond. Finally, even the most featureless and unexciting exterior can be brought to life with a sense of humour and a lick of paint!

When a row of houses or cottages all have colour-washed rendering, the contrasts between the individual properties can look delightful, especially if the owners have got together and designed a colour plan of the street that works to everyone's satisfaction. This style of decoration is somewhat reminiscent of the eighteenth century, when rendered houses and cottages often had brightly painted façades, popular colours being deep pink, russet, ochre and even aquamarine – with windows framed in black, white or a light tint.

Any paintwork on brick houses should work with – not compete against – itself. Old rosy red bricks and more modern orangey ones will profit visually from the refreshing contrast of white paintwork. This can extend to the front door, although both deep blue and deep green can also look very smart at the entrance. Grey brickwork also responds well to white paintwork teamed with deep green, ochre or terracotta-red. Neutral brick or render can be livened up by a combination of white and black, or by mid-toned smoke blue or muted terracotta spiced with white.

An old house with unusual combinations of exterior construction, such as stone inset with brick or external half-timbering, should be given the simplest exterior paint treatments, but check before painting any brick that it is suitable for such treatment; there are more bricks that cannot be painted than can. Garish colours should be avoided at all cost – they don't lend themselves to older houses. However, many modern houses, especially some of the developments of the sixties with their limited use of exterior detail, are able to take the boldest of colours on their façades.

PAINTED WINDOWS

Right: 'You'll pass a blue house on your left, you can't miss it!' With it's rendered walls painted a bright blue sharpened in white, this house will surely figure in many sets of traffic directions. You could say this is colour used to memorable and stunning effect.

Looking from left to right, a fine yellow line gives effective definition to the moulded outer frame of a sash window. In the next picture, pale stone masonry paint and black railings repeat the classic formula of stucco rendering on eighteenth and early nineteenth century houses. Next, sunshine bright shutters and decorative flower boxes dress up windows in a vivid Mediterranean style. Finally, a sultry contrast of turquoise and pink give emphasis to special features. Glazing bars are picked out in pink, shutters in blue, and the half-louvred door is delicately outlined in both.

**The Right Paint**

• Paint has been used for centuries to distinguish the house in its landscape. The first pigments were crushed charcoal and earth tints such as yellow and red ochre. By the eighteenth century, more advanced chemical pigments gave a wider range of subtle colours including pale greens as well as neutral stone colours and variants of peach, apricot and yellow.

• Now we can choose Dulux Weathershield Masonry Paint for exterior walls and Dulux Weathershield Exterior Gloss – the most advanced formulas and balanced choice of colour ever available.

Left: a nineteenth century Gothic Revival house has its rendering tinted a pale hopsack green. The glazing bars of the sash windows are picked out in white to match the decorative cut-out bargeboarding which trims the edge of the gable and forms the principal focus of the facade.

# PRACTICAL

## MATTERS

There's never been a better time to pick up a paintbrush, whether you're a regular or a novice decorator. Why? Because today the range of products specifically designed for DIY use is wider than ever before. In Britain the DIY market is so important that manufacturers are making their merchandise as quick and easy to use as possible. The newest versions of the paints and varnishes that once required practised skill to apply now make home decorating simple for everybody and give good results, even for the least adept, while products like quick-drying wood primer/undercoat or non-drip gloss (which doesn't require undercoat at all when used on previously painted wood) are great time-savers as well. The colour ranges available are selected to reflect furnishing trends, so your choice of product need not limit your colour scheme. 'Solid' emulsion comes in a range of soft whites that have proved extremely popular, and you'll find non-drip gloss in all the popular shades too.

The traditional materials are still there for those who want results to reach a professional standard. Once you have gained experience and confidence using paints like non-drip gloss, you can progress to liquid gloss, which gives an unbeatable shine, and exterior products like masonry paint. Many products which were once exclusive to the decorating trade are now available to all – such as Weathershield Exterior Gloss which gives two years' added protection to exterior woodwork. There's a knack to applying these products, which this section sets out to explain, but provided you follow the correct procedure and don't skip or rush any of the steps, you should achieve successful results.

As well as straightforward paint finishes there are many decorative alternatives to consider. Satinwood, for example, is a new 'trim' finish, especially developed to give a sheen to interior woodwork and radiators and to complement the colour of the walls. Non-drip varnish enables amateurs to achieve a professional finish with a product which was once notoriously difficult to manipulate. Then there are paint treatments such as sponging and stencilling which introduce pattern to painted walls. There's no need to use specialized products for the basic techniques, which can be carried out with straightforward emulsion as well as oil-based paint. For the techniques shown here, all you need is a sponge, a bunch of rags, a roller or a ready-made stencil, available from art shops or DIY stores. Nor do you need special skills. Treatments like these are surprisingly easy – and effective – to create, and an ideal way to brighten up existing paintwork if you don't want to repaint the entire room.

All set to go! Home decorating isn't difficult, but don't neglect the groundwork. Remove or cover furniture and carpets before you start.

To get the best out of today's decorating materials, do take time to read the instructions carefully. Improvements are constantly being introduced, so the way you applied paint yesterday may not be right for the product you buy today. Thorough preparation is also extremely important; don't skimp on this stage, tedious though it may be. When you've spent time creating a colour scheme and money on decorating materials, it's worth spending a little more of each on the groundwork which is essential for a fine finish.

**P**reparation is important because paint and wallpaper will only adhere to a clean, dry surface – it affects the lifespan as well as the looks of the materials you choose.

## EQUIPMENT

For basic preparation work you will need:
● a stripping knife or scraper with a wide blade for lifting wallpaper and areas of flaking paint
● an angled putty knife for filling narrow cracks and crevices
● a filling knife with a flexible blade for patching average-sized cracks
● a wire brush for scoring stubborn wall-coverings to allow the detergent solution to seep in and loosen the adhesive
● a sanding block, which can be made from cork, timber, rubber, or an offcut of wood
● abrasive paper (silicon carbide paper is more expensive but can be used wet or dry)
● a bucket and sponge plus detergent or sugar soap solution for washing down walls and loosening wallpaper
● a stepladder

## EXTRAS

● a wallpaper stripper (which you can get from hire shops) is helpful if you have large areas of stubborn wallcovering to remove

## PROTECTION

Remove as much furniture as possible, group the rest in the centre of the room and cover completely. Take down curtains, blinds and light fittings and take up carpets where practicable, or cover with dust sheets. Remember to provide work clothing for yourself but avoid jumpers which may shed fibres on to newly painted surfaces. Keep a pair of old shoes for use when decorating and remove them at the door, to prevent paint being trodden into your carpets or other flooring.

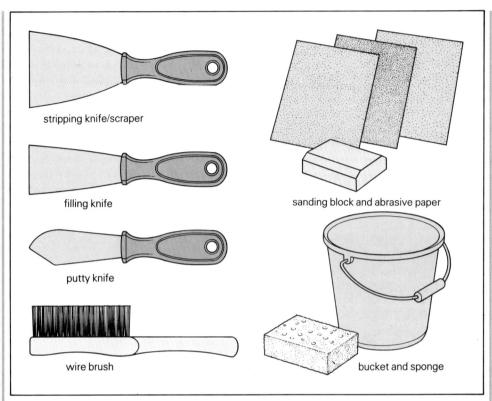

stripping knife/scraper

filling knife

putty knife

wire brush

sanding block and abrasive paper

bucket and sponge

Above: make sure you have all the tools you need for preparation before you start. Buy the best you can afford – you'll need them for all decorating, both inside and out.

Below: clear the room completely if possible before you start decorating. Take down shelves and curtain poles as well as soft furnishings and cover what can't be moved.

## PREPARATION

**Flaking paint** should be removed by scraping and sanding. If the walls are powdery and dusty, apply a coat of stabilizing solution (such as Dulux Primer Sealer) before redecorating.

**New, clean plaster** needs an initial 'mist' coat of emulsion paint, thinned with water, which acts as a primer or sealer.

**Wallpaper** should be stripped as new paper or paint may cause poorly adhering areas to lift. You can paint over lining paper, the backing of paper-backed wallcoverings and relief wallcoverings designed to be covered by paint provided they are sound, but never paint or paper over wallpaper that's dark, water-resistant or peeling. Dry-strippable wallcoverings (e.g. vinyls and some washable wallpapers) are easiest to remove. Pull up a corner by the skirting: the surface should then strip away quite easily. Otherwise apply detergent solution from the top of the wall down so that the water penetrates the wallpaper (take care not to overwet plasterboard which may swell) and remove carefully with the stripping knife; you may need to score the surface with a wire brush, particularly if the wallpaper has been overpainted.

**Cracks** in plaster and chips in wood must be filled and sanded level with the surround. The cheapest filler for walls is a cellulose powder that's mixed with water to the required consistency. For cracks where surfaces join and for wood as well as plaster, choose a flexible multi-purpose filler. Hairline cracks in plaster should be opened out so that the filler can get a proper grip (see right). Chips in protruding corners and small holes should be treated with several layers of filler. Build it up so that the area stands proud, and then sand flush with the wall.

Now lightly sand paintwork, radiators and walls where oil-based paint (such as gloss or eggshell) has been used to provide a key for the new paint. Wash walls and woodwork with detergent solution, rinse with clean water and allow to dry.

- **Distemper** is a powdery wall finish that rubs away and neither paint nor paper will adhere to it. Wash it off with a sponge, changing the water frequently, and finish with a coat of primer sealer like Dulux Primer Sealer.

- **Efflorescence** (white salts on the surface of the wall) occurs when plaster is drying out. Brush away and decorate with emulsion paint when the salts have ceased to appear. Don't use wallpaper or oil-based paints for 12 months, otherwise you may get mould growth.

- **Mould** (black fungus on the wall) must be cured before redecorating. If it is formed by condensation, treat the mould with a solution of one part domestic bleach to four parts water, leave for 48 hours, then wash off with clear water. Repeat the process if necessary, and try to improve ventilation. If it is caused by rising or penetrating damp, seek professional advice from a builder or surveyor.

**1** Open out a hairline crack with a stripping knife or a putty knife, then dust off with a dusting brush.

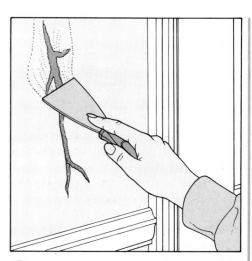

**2** Stop up cracks with proprietary filler, applied with a flexible filling knife, and sand smooth when it is dry.

**3** Rub down existing paint on woodwork to provide a key for the next coat, using abrasive paper, then dust off.

**4** Wash the walls, working from the bottom up to prevent streaks, then rinse well and allow to dry before redecorating.

Although there is a bewildering variety of brands and descriptions on the market, there are only two main types of paint: gloss and emulsions.

**Oil-based paints** (sometimes called solvent-based paints) include liquid and non-drip gloss, undercoat, oil-based mid-sheen paint (Dulux Satinwood or eggshell), and finishes such as enamel and lacquer. Gloss paints are generally used for wood and metal, but eggshell and Satinwood paints may be used for walls as well as woodwork and radiators. Choose Satinwood for areas of wear like the hall, kitchen and bathroom, or to emphasize the pattern of relief wallcoverings. They can all be thinned or cleaned with white spirit, though some gloss and Satinwood paints can be washed from brushes with strong detergent and water immediately after use – be sure to follow the manufacturer's instructions, given on the tin.

**Emulsion paints** are all water-soluble, so brushes can be cleaned with warm water and washing up liquid. Emulsion paint is designed for walls and ceilings, and modern varieties contain vinyl to improve wear. The terms satin, or silk, and matt describe the degree of shine. Shinier emulsions are easier to clean than matt but they also magnify irregularities in the wall. Matt finish emulsion has a velvety appearance that looks attractive in living rooms and bedrooms. Both varieties are available in the non-drip 'solid' emulsion pioneered by Dulux – this comes complete with a paint tray and is designed for use with a roller.

Paint ranges are available for DIY use (like Dulux Colour Collections) or for the trade. If you can't find a shade to suit, look at those produced by a tinting machine; Dulux Colours by Matchmaker offers a choice of over 550 different hues. Gloss paints are sold in 0.5, 1, and 2.5 litre cans; and emulsion paints are available in 1, 2.5 and 5 litre cans.

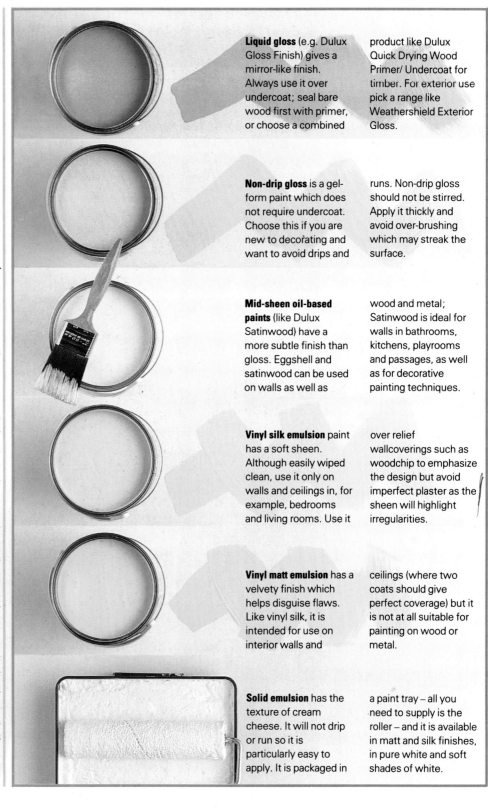

**Liquid gloss** (e.g. Dulux Gloss Finish) gives a mirror-like finish. Always use it over undercoat; seal bare wood first with primer, or choose a combined product like Dulux Quick Drying Wood Primer/ Undercoat for timber. For exterior use pick a range like Weathershield Exterior Gloss.

**Non-drip gloss** is a gel-form paint which does not require undercoat. Choose this if you are new to decorating and want to avoid drips and runs. Non-drip gloss should not be stirred. Apply it thickly and avoid over-brushing which may streak the surface.

**Mid-sheen oil-based paints** (like Dulux Satinwood) have a more subtle finish than gloss. Eggshell and satinwood can be used on walls as well as wood and metal; Satinwood is ideal for walls in bathrooms, kitchens, playrooms and passages, as well as for decorative painting techniques.

**Vinyl silk emulsion** paint has a soft sheen. Although easily wiped clean, use it only on walls and ceilings in, for example, bedrooms and living rooms. Use it over relief wallcoverings such as woodchip to emphasize the design but avoid imperfect plaster as the sheen will highlight irregularities.

**Vinyl matt emulsion** has a velvety finish which helps disguise flaws. Like vinyl silk, it is intended for use on interior walls and ceilings (where two coats should give perfect coverage) but it is not at all suitable for painting on wood or metal.

**Solid emulsion** has the texture of cream cheese. It will not drip or run so it is particularly easy to apply. It is packaged in a paint tray – all you need to supply is the roller – and it is available in matt and silk finishes, in pure white and soft shades of white.

Right: the bathroom presents special problems, needing a paint that stands up to condensation and changing temperatures. Satinwood paints are designed to resist the steamy atmosphere, providing an elegant but hardworking paint finish.

Below: washable and resilient, Satinwood paint is excellent for the kitchen where surfaces are exposed to heat, condensation and the spills and splashes inevitably connected with cooking.

Right: the soft smoothness of vinyl matt emulsion has a restful quality ideal for bedroom decor. This subtle warm pink creates a fresh effect combined with cleverly co-ordinated soft furnishings.

Take your time when you choose equipment for painting. Run brushes over your hand and discard any that moult profusely, and assess the weight of rollers and wall brushes until you find one which feels comfortable to use – don't automatically pick the largest to speed up the work. Remember to clean equipment immediately after use and hang brushes up to dry. If you want a break, place the brushes or roller in water so they don't dry out; brush off on a board before painting again.

**1** roller plus long hair lamb's wool sleeve and tray
**2** short-pile mohair roller sleeve for vinyl silk emulsion and solid emulsion paint
**3** 75mm paint brush (useful for doors)
**4** 50mm paint brush (for skirtings)
**5** 25mm paint brush (for window frames)
**6** angled 19mm cutting-in brush for filling in

window glazing bars
**7** 100mm wall brush for use with emulsion or masonry paint
**8 & 9** paint pads in various widths for broad and narrow surfaces
**10** sash paint pad for window frames and awkward areas
**11** paint kettle for decanting paint from the tin and S hook for suspending it

**Cleaning Brushes**
● Emulsion paint can be removed with detergent solution but oil-based paints usually require white spirit. If brushes need soaking, drill a hole through the handle, push a nail through and suspend over a jar of brush cleaner. Rinse and hang up to dry.

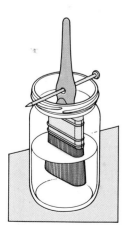

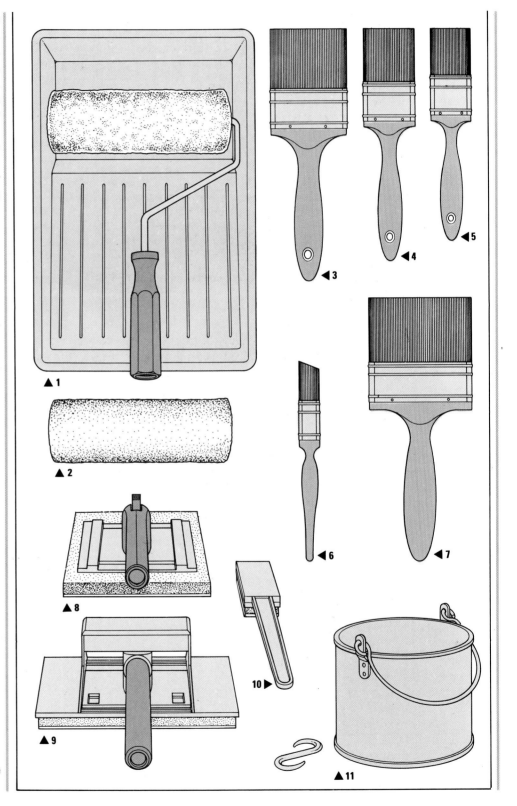

**Brushes** are the traditional – and most versatile – form of painting equipment. Choose natural hog's hair bristles, which are expensive, but they do carry more paint. The bristles should be tapered at the tip so that you can smooth the surface for a fine finish, a process called 'laying off' which is particularly important when using gloss. You'll need a range of widths for use on metal and wood (75, 50 and 25mm are a good choice, and the latter is also ideal to fill in the margins of walls when using a wall brush or roller) plus a narrow cutting-in brush for window glazing bars. A long-handled crevice brush is also helpful for painting behind radiators and pipes. Most brushes are designed for use on metal and wood but choose a wall brush for emulsion if you feel comfortable with this method. Don't choose an extra-wide brush unless you have the strength to use it – 100mm is usually sufficient. Hold a wide brush by the stock (the part between the bristles and the handle) and a narrow brush like a pencil for proper control. Dip the brush into the paint until the bristles are half-covered, then dab the brush on the side of the container to remove excess paint. Keep brushes moist when you break for lunch by standing them in a pot of water; always clean them at the end of the day with the appropriate solvent (usually detergent and water for emulsion, white spirit for gloss) and hang them up to dry.

**Rollers** are the most popular tools for painting walls. Widths vary from 175 to 300mm but you may find wide rollers too unwieldy. Double frame rollers (where the sleeve is attached to the handle at both sides) are useful when painting ceilings because you can exert a steady pressure even when using an extension handle, but they won't reach into corners as success-fully as the single frame type. You can also buy small angled rollers which, like crevice brushes, are intended for painting behind obstacles. A variety of sleeves is available but it's advisable to avoid foam which may

## DULUX PAINT CHART

(For varnish see page 107, for exterior paints see pages 120-123)

| Product | Coverage (per litre) | Recoatable |
|---|---|---|
| Dulux Gloss Finish (liquid gloss) | 17 sq m | 16 hrs |
| Dulux Non-Drip Gloss | 12 sq m | 16 hrs |
| Dulux Undercoat | 15 sq m | 16 hrs |
| Dulux Quick Drying Wood Primer/Undercoat | 11-13 sq m | 2 hrs |
| Dulux Quick Drying Metal Primer | 10 sq m | 6 hrs |
| Dulux All Purpose Primer | 7 sq m (wood) | 16 hrs |
| | 11 sq m (metal) | |
| Dulux Wood Primer White | 11-15 sq m | 16 hrs |
| Dulux Primer Sealer | 9 sq m | 24 hrs |
| Dulux Satinwood | 16 sq m | 16 hrs |
| Dulux Vinyl Silk Emulsion (liquid and solid) | 11 sq m | 6 hrs |
| Dulux Vinyl Matt Emulsion (liquid and solid) | 12 sq m | 6 hrs |

This is a general guide. Coverage will vary with the absorbency of the surface, drying times depend on climatic conditions.

cause the paint to spatter. Lamb's wool is a good general purpose sleeve, especially suited to vinyl matt emulsion and textured surfaces, but choose a short pile mohair sleeve for use with eggshell, vinyl silk or solid emulsion paint. Rollers are used in conjunction with a paint tray. Pour paint into the base of the tray and roll the sleeve backwards and forwards in the paint until it is coated. Remove excess paint on the ribs of the tray.

**Paint pads** are useful for beginners as they are easy to manipulate, but the quality of finish may not be as good as that obtained with a roller. Some pads are hinged at the handle to make it easier to paint round obstacles. A number of sizes up to 200mm in width are available, including narrow 25mm wide 'sash' pads for painting window frames or for cutting-in. Like rollers, paint pads are used, and often sold, with a paint tray.

It's essential to use the right paint and the right tools for good-looking and long-lasting results. This kitchen/dining room receives maximum protection for large areas of gloss-painted woodwork which will resist knocks and condensation. Varnish provides an attractive floor and the walls are painted in vinyl matt emulsion to contrast with the shiny surfaces.

- Make a note of the quantities and number of coats you need when decorating a room and file it for reference.
- Vacuum the room after preparation work is complete to prevent dust and fluff from sticking to the new paintwork.
- If the room has a polished floor, remove any wax from the skirtings before you decorate or the paint will not adhere.
- Remember that oil-based paints such as gloss and Satinwood take several days to harden completely. Don't put books and ornaments on to newly painted shelves.
- Don't stir non-drip gloss or solid emulsion or they will liquefy.
- Liquid paint should be stirred with a beating motion until any sediment or oil is incorporated and the paint is smooth.
- Work in a well-ventilated room to disperse fumes from oil-based paints.

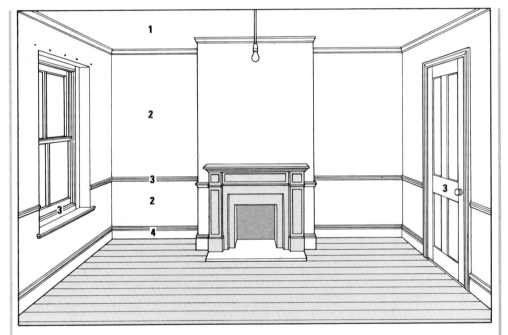

There's nothing intrinsically difficult about painting a ceiling. The only big problem is that it's very tiring working with your hands above your head for any length of time, so it's important to set up a stable work station (see right) which reduces the amount of stretching you have to do. Take frequent breaks, but try to complete painting in one day or you may be left with a tide mark where the paint dries out. Use a roller for speed but remember that the ceiling may need a second coat unless you are merely freshening it with the same colour.

Start by stripping old wallpaper. If lining paper is sound and firmly stuck down, it can be painted; if it has been overpainted several times, it's best to take it down as the weight of the paint will weaken the adhesive.

Next, wash the ceiling with detergent solution, rinse and allow to dry. You will need to treat residue distemper with primer sealer; treat nicotine or smoke stains with alkali-resisting primer. Don't skip this step even if the ceiling looks relatively clean because any grease or dirt on the surface will impair the new paint's adhesion. A window-cleaning squeegee or a sponge mop makes this task easier. You can use extension handles (or a broom handle) with paint rollers, but this may affect control; it's better to work nearer the ceiling.

Fill cracks in the normal way and sand level. If the ceiling has a textured finish, use a damp sponge to wipe away the excess filler or stipple it to try to match the texture.

Ceilings in older houses are often higher than average and can take a deeper colour than the usual white. Where light is limited, opt for a soft white or a pastel, and pick out mouldings in pure brilliant white for contrast. If there is a picture rail, treat the area of wall above it in the same way as the ceiling or, if wall and ceiling are similar in colour, fill it with a paint or paper frieze.

Tackle mouldings and ceiling decorations before you embark on the main area. Give them an initial coat of paint (emulsion is best, particularly for fragile ornaments), then

Follow the correct painting procedure to ensure that any slips of the brush or roller are erased by the subsequent stage.

**1** Begin by painting the highest point: the ceiling. Give any decorations an initial coat before painting the ceiling and complete later.

**2** Next paint the walls, working away from the light from the top downwards.

**3** Woodwork (window frames, picture rail and doors in that order) is painted next if you are decorating with paint but NOT if you are papering the walls when all woodwork should be painted after the ceiling.

**4** Finish by painting the skirting. 'Cut in' with a small paintbrush at door and window frames and wall margins where rollers will not reach.

paint the rest of the ceiling as shown (right). Take special care not to overlap the mouldings if you are using a deep colour here. Finish the ceiling with a second coat if required, then complete the mouldings and decorations. Remember to protect your hair with a scarf and your eyes with an eyeshield.

Vinyl matt emulsion paint is a favourite choice for ceilings, except in rooms which have vinyl silk walls where you may wish to avoid a change of finish. If the ceiling has a textured finish (e.g. Artex), coverage may be improved by using a lamb's wool sleeve on the roller to reach into the crevices. One word of warning – NEVER use oil-based paint (gloss or eggshell) on polystyrene tiles as this creates a fire hazard.

Decorate the ceiling first, then deal with the walls and finish by painting woodwork and radiators. Follow this system even in a complicated area like this hall, where the archways should be painted at the same time as you tackle the walls and the mouldings picked out in conjunction with the paintwork.

Work a comfortable distance from the ceiling, using a board supported by two pairs of steps, or steps and a hop-up as shown.

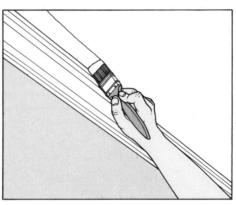

1 Paint a narrow strip round the edge of the ceiling as the roller will not reach this far. This process is known as 'cutting in'.

2 Now paint a strip parallel to this line with the roller, leaving a gap between the two. Don't overload the roller or the paint will drip.

3 When you come to the end wall, reverse the direction and join the two strips, then run the roller over again.

4 Reload the roller and start a new strip parallel to the first. Work in this way until the ceiling is complete.

The easiest way to transform a room is to paint the walls. In a couple of hours you can change its appearance from neutral to bright and from dark to pale – or vice versa. The quality of finish depends on adequate preparation, so set aside sufficient time for this important first stage. Although it may take far longer than painting, it is vital if you're to achieve acceptable results.

Allow two coats of emulsion paint for effective coverage. This should be enough even if you are changing dark to light, provided you use a reputable brand. The one exception is when you are painting bare plaster, when you should apply a preliminary coat of emulsion thinned with water to seal the wall. If you want to use an oil-based finish (such as eggshell) on the walls, prime bare, dry plaster first with an alkali-resisting primer. Bear in mind it can be difficult to tolerate the fumes produced by the solvent in oil-based paints when they are used in large quantities, so choose emulsion for walls where possible. You will certainly need an oil-based paint for decorative paint techniques (such as sponging and ragging) because it dries more slowly than emulsion and gives you more time to create the effect, but it's perfectly possible to apply oil-based paint over a base coat of vinyl silk emulsion, thus reducing the quantity you require.

Begin painting away from the light, from the top of the wall down. (Remember to cut in with a small brush at the edges of the wall and round door and window frames and light switches.) Don't overload the brush, roller or paint pad in an effort to speed things up; this will simply cause drips and runs. As emulsion paint dries quickly and is ready for recoating in four to six hours, never stop painting in the centre of a wall, or the resulting join will be difficult to disguise. Finally, try to paint during daylight; artificial light casts confusing shadows and these may lead to errors which are all too obvious next day.

**Paint pads** are easy for beginners to use. Work in bands along the wall, thinning the paint if needed.

**Rollers** are quick to use but give a mottled finish. Apply the paint in a criss-cross direction to cover the wall.

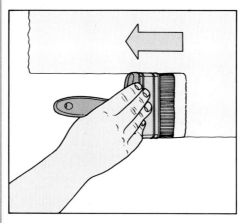

**Brushes** need more expertise. Cut in at the corners as usual before painting a horizontal band with the wall brush.

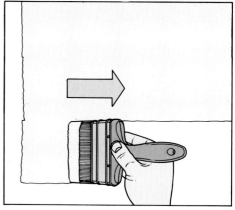

When the strip is an arm's span long, broaden the band with a return stroke of the brush, working downwards.

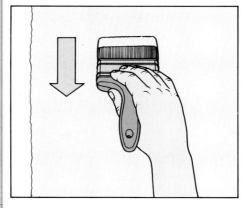

'Lay off' with light vertical strokes. Finish with a downward stroke when painting the top of the wall.

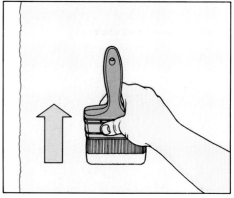

When painting the lower part, finish with an upward stroke. Always hold the brush by the stock for proper control.

ack of preparation is to blame for most disappointments in decorating. In many cases, the best remedy is to sand down the paint if necessary, wash the walls and start again.

**Blisters?** You have painted the wall before it was dry, or it may be damp, or you have used emulsion over gloss.

**Brushmarks?** Don't overload the brush, or spread the paint too thinly. Make sure that bristles are soft; if they have hardened, soak the brush in a proprietary cleaner. If it's past saving, throw the brush away.

**Crazing?** You have not cleaned and rinsed the surface thoroughly enough first, or the top coat (particularly an oil-based paint) has been applied before the base coat is dry.

**Dimpled paint?** Again, you have probably not cleaned the surface thoroughly enough first. It may also result from condensation forming as the paint dries – another fault common to oil-based paints – in which case, keep the room warm, well-ventilated and the temperature steady while the paint dries.

**Flaking?** This is caused by many things: poor adhesion due to surface contamination; damp; using emulsion over gloss; too many coats of paint; or a powdery surface. If it is the latter, wash and rinse walls thoroughly after filling and sanding and then brush down any large patches. If the wall is still flaky, sand well and treat with a coat of primer sealer.

**Runs?** You have overloaded the brush or roller. Try a non-drip product, and take your time!

**Bittiness?** This occurs when dust is trapped beneath the paint. Thorough preparation before you start painting should prevent this, but if the problem is severe, sand, wash thoroughly and repaint.

**Uneven coverage?** You may have spread the paint too thinly or tried to cover in one coat. Alternatively, you may have failed to prime patches of bare plaster, which are more absorbent than painted walls.

ON THE RIGHT LINES

Black, white or blue, diagonal, horizontal, or used to create a frieze and define a doorway – stripes do more than decorate a room, they seem to alter its proportions too.

tripes are smart and will help to increase the apparent height or width of a room. Stripes must appear straight, so use a plumb bob and line and mark vertical stripes lightly in chalk or pencil. For horizontal stripes, measure the wall from the ceiling in five places, joining the marks to form a guideline. Step back, then make alterations; the line may look crooked if the walls are out of true. Fix masking tape along the edges of each stripe, then paint the base coat in emulsion – masking tape may damage a matt finish. When dry, remove the tape carefully.

nly an oil-based paint can resist the wear and tear on woodwork. Doors, window frames, skirting and furniture have to withstand rough treatment, so protect them with the toughest paints available.

**Gloss** (liquid or non-drip) gives the highest degree of shine, ideal for areas where you want the contrast of bright colour or pure white.

**Mid-sheen finishes** like eggshell and Satin-wood have a soft, silky look for schemes where you want woodwork to blend with the walls. Gloss and mid-sheen paints may be used on radiators and interior metal.

**Varnish** will protect and preserve the appearance of natural wood. Coloured finishes are also available both in timber shades and bright colours which emphasize the grain. For special effects, you can use clear varnish over emulsion or decorative paint treatments, but be warned, it may cause discoloration and the varnish must be removed before you repaint.

## PREPARATION

First remove any door 'furniture' – handles, key fobs and finger plates – and scrape old or loose putty from around the window panes. Existing paint in good condition makes a perfect base for the new coat; simply sand it lightly to provide a key, then dust off. Lumpy or flaking paint should be sanded well to obtain a smooth surface before cleaning and any bare areas sealed with a wood or all-purpose primer. If the paint is in poor condition, strip it completely and start again.

**Primer** should be applied to all bare wood before painting to seal the surface. For interior wood, choose wood primer, an all-purpose (or universal) primer or a dual purpose primer/undercoat. Remember to prime the bottom edges of new doors and window rebates where putty has been removed – areas which are often overlooked.

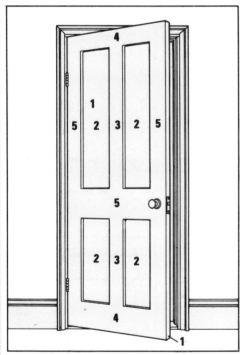

**Follow this order of painting – it will help you to avoid smudges and obtain the best results:**
1 mouldings
2 panels
3 central verticals
4 top and bottom

horizontals
5 inner and outer verticals, edges and frame.
**Remember to paint the rim of the door to match the room it opens into so that it blends with the decor.**

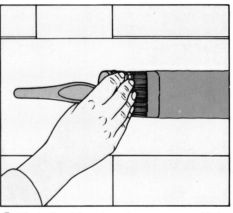

1 Dip the brush into the paint to cover one-third of the bristle area. Now paint the first strip, working along the grain.

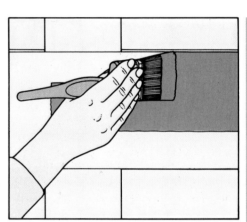

2 Without reloading the brush, paint a second strip parallel to the first. Blend the two together so that they overlap.

3 Dip the brush in the paint and apply paint across the grain so that the area is completely and evenly covered.

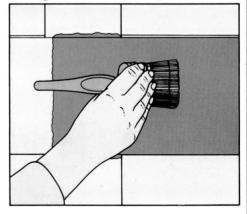

4 Finish by 'laying off' with featherlight strokes along the grain to eliminate brushmarks and obtain a fine finish.

**Knots** on new wood should be touched in with knotting solution to prevent discoloration. If brown rings appear on painted wood, sand the area down to bare wood, treat the knot, and prime before applying undercoat and gloss in the usual way.

**Cracks** must be primed before they are filled. Choose flexible multi-purpose filler for painted wood but opt for a wood filler to blend with natural wood if you intend to varnish: you may need to tint it with wood stain for an exact match.

**Undercoat** blots out previous colours and provides a base for liquid gloss. The range of colours here is limited because single tone works with a number of top coats – use the colour recommended on the can of the top coat you plan to use.

## APPLICATION

Liquid gloss should always be applied over undercoat. Although care should be taken not to overload the brush – only a third of the bristle area should be covered with paint – runs are always the result of uneven application. Don't wipe the bristles against the rim of the can – lumps may form and fall inside the tin. Dip the brush in the tin or paint kettle, then dab it against the side of the container to remove excess paint. Always stir liquid gloss well to incorporate oil and sediment. If lumps appear, strain the paint through a stocking or a fine sieve. To prevent a skin forming in a half-used tin of gloss, close the lid tightly and then invert the can. Don't use a screwdriver to open the tin as this distorts the lid – use a bottle opener instead.

**Non-drip gloss** needs no undercoat. It should not be applied too thinly or brushed out too enthusiastically.

**Mid-sheen finish** (eggshell and Satinwood) requires undercoat when used on woodwork: apply as for liquid gloss.

Whichever paint you choose, allow two coats for coverage. Leave woodwork to dry overnight and remember that it will take several days to harden.

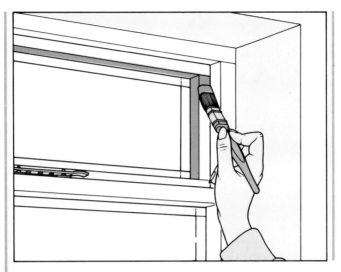

Paint on the window panes looks amateurish and spoils the view! Although many people use masking tape to ensure a good edge, it isn't ideal because it leaves an edge that is prone to condensation and flaking. To ensure a good clean edge, use a hand-held paint shield, or 'George', instead and a narrow paint brush or cutting-in brush; overlap the window pane by a millimetre or so to form a weatherproof seal.

**Casement Windows**
First paint any glazing bars on the fixed window.

Next paint the opening casement. (Outside edges should match exterior paint.)

Finally the main window frame and the interior sill should be painted.

**Sash Windows**
Open as shown. Paint the frame rim and lower sash.

Pull back the lower sash, then pull up the top sash and finish painting it.

Paint the bottom sash and the frame, taking care to avoid the sash cords.

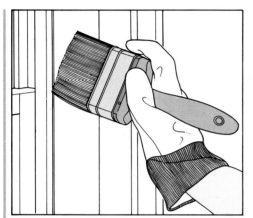

**Liquid paint stripper** should be applied with a brush, dabbed well into crevices and left for the required time.

When the paint has softened sufficiently it will bubble and can be removed with a stripping knife and shavehook.

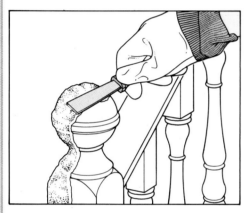

**Paste stripper** is easier to manipulate on vertical surfaces. Apply it thickly with a filling knife for maximum effect.

Leave for the suggested time and then carefully peel both paste stripper and paint from the surface beneath.

**A hot air gun** which uses indirect heat is less likely to scorch than a blow torch which has a naked flame.

**Shavehooks** are triangular or combination (with curved and straight edges) in shape to remove paint from awkward crevices.

## STRIPPING WOOD

**Chemical stripper** is available as liquid or paste, which has the advantage of clinging to vertical surfaces (stand furniture legs in saucers to collect the residue if using liquid stripper). Be prepared to apply several layers and to wait (anything from 15 minutes to eight hours) before the paint softens.

**Heat stripping** has been revolutionized by the electrically-powered hot air gun, now with variable temperatures from 100° to 300°C. Work from the bottom of the wood up so that rising heat softens the paint above, taking care not to scorch the wood, and wear gloves for protection.

**Dry stripping** involves using a shavehook plus a stripping knife to remove loose paint.

**Sanding** finishes the process, and should be done in the direction of the grain if you plan to varnish afterwards. Hand-sanding produces a fine finish, but it's quicker to use an electrically-powered orbital sander or a belt sander (see over) for large areas. A disc sander attachment for a drill copes with rough work but may score the wood.

Use clear varnish in gloss, matt or satin finish to protect, or a natural wood shade, as here, to modify existing colour.

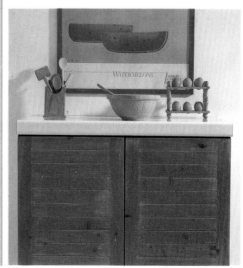

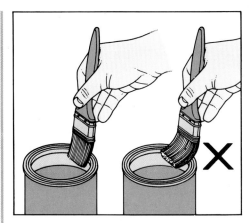

**1** Always use a new paintbrush or a special varnish brush when varnishing and take care not to bend the bristles.

**2** Always working along the grain, pre-seal the surface if necessary, sand, dust off, then apply the first coat.

**3** On narrow or vertical surfaces apply the varnish with a single sweeping stroke to cover the area.

**4** Brush the varnish out fully to the edges, working to each side in turn, with firm, steady strokes.

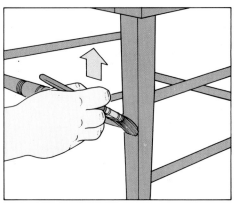

**5** Finish by 'laying off' with a single upward stroke to eliminate trickles of varnish which may form at the sides.

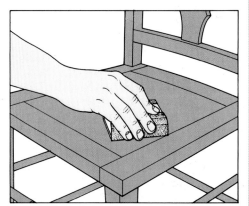

**6** When it is dry, rub down lightly with fine abrasive paper and dust off before applying a second coat.

**V**arnish protects timber while allowing the beauty of the grain to show through, and provides a durable surface which is more resistant to dirt and damp. Dulux Varnish is suitable for wood and cork on all interior surfaces, from furniture to floors, but check the instructions on the tin if you choose another brand because not all have the resistance to abrasion a flooring product requires. Generally, the higher the gloss, the better the durability, so take care when choosing a matt or semi-gloss.

Remember that varnish requires a finer finish than paint. Existing paint should be stripped with care and if there are discre-pancies in the colour of the wood, you will need to bleach it (using special wood bleach) or stain it to an even shade before you varnish, while filler should be chosen or tinted to blend with the surround. Varnish can be applied over existing varnish provided it is sound, sanded, dusted off and clean; defective varnish should be removed completely. Bare wood and cork should be sealed with a preliminary coat of clear gloss varnish diluted with up to 10 per cent white spirit. Sand lightly and dust off before applying a second coat. One or two coats of varnish are normally suffi-cient, except for floors which require three or four for maximum durability.

● Clear varnish gives protection without change of colour. It is available in gloss (usually the most hard-wearing), satin and matt finish and now in a non-drip formula which makes it easier to apply. Natural wood shades combine wood dye and varnish in one and are also available in non-drip finish. Use them to enhance or to change the colour of the wood, as well as to protect it. Remember that the shade will vary with the number of coats and original wood colour. Coloured varnish in translucent shades offers the positive colour of paint plus the transparency of varnish. The effect will depend on the original colour of the wood and the number of coats applied.

**W**hy buy carpet when a wood floor can look so good? Once sanded and sealed, floorboards provide an impervious and durable surface that's just right for halls and dining rooms, and even for living rooms and bedrooms too. Although it's an economical process, not all floorboards repay the effort involved. Thin, patched or uneven boards rarely make a satisfactory surface, while a stained border may result in some difference in colour even when bleached. Boards more than 3mm apart are best taken up and the floor relayed.

## EQUIPMENT

You will need:
- a nail punch for recessing nails
- fillets of wood and wood filler for cracks
- a plane for smoothing
- a power sander with dust bag (from hire shops) with three grades of abrasive
- dust mask and goggles
- a belt sander for treating the edges
- a shavehook
- abrasive paper and sanding block
- white spirit
- sufficient varnish for 3-4 coats
- 75mm paintbrush

## PREPARATION

First tap down any protruding nails so that they will not catch on the abrasive fitted to the power sander. Fill substantial gaps between the boards with wedge-shaped pieces of timber to match the floor. (Spread wood adhesive on both sides, tap into place with a hammer, protecting the surface with an offcut of wood, and plane smooth.) Stop up small cracks with wood filler, stained to match the surround.

## SANDING

Hire a power sander with a dust bag to treat floorboards. Sanding is heavy work, so allow sufficient time to complete the

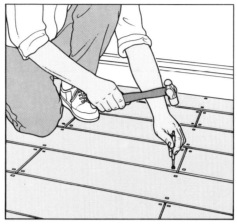

**1** Punch all nail heads and countersink screws below the surface before sanding to prevent them catching the abrasive.

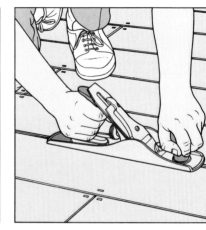

**2** Fill gaps with fillets of wood and plane them flush with the surround. Stain to match the existing floor if necessary.

**3** Run the power sander diagonally across the boards to flatten them and to remove ingrained dirt and polish.

**4** Use a belt sander at the perimeter of the room where the power sander cannot reach, taking care to sand with the grain.

**Types of floor**
- If your floorboards aren't worth sanding, consider a new timber floor. All floors (except planks laid direct to joists) need a sub-floor. Lay hardboard rough side up and condition it for a few days in the room where it will be used.
- Parquet should be

left to the professionals, but some other types are ideal for DIY use.
- Mosaic flooring consists of panels made from small rectangles of wood arranged in a basketweave design. (These separate into individual 'fingers' for fitting round

obstacles.) Lay mosaic like floor tiles over a hardboard sub-floor and leave a 12mm expansion gap filled with cork or covered by moulding. As the pattern prevents sanding along the grain, use an orbital sander at a 45° angle before varnishing.
- Wood strip tongue

and groove flooring can be clipped, glued, or 'secret nailed' through the tongue. Lay over a hardboard sub-floor and leave an expansion gap as before, staggering the joins to prevent weakness. Sand lightly with an orbital sander, clean and varnish.

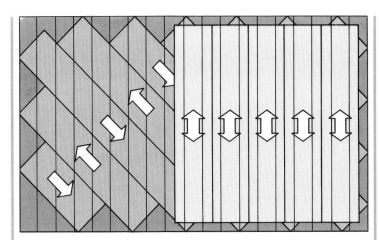

**1** Sand the boards first diagonally and then along the grain, overlapping each strip by about 75mm. Remember to switch off the power sander when you reach the wall to avoid scratching the boards as you turn.

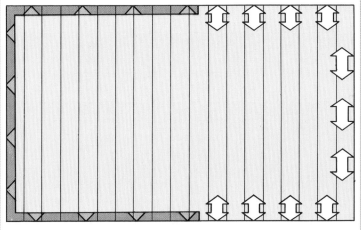

**2** Remember to always sand along the grain when treating the edges of the room with the small belt sander – don't automatically work towards the wall or the result will look patchy.

Sanded floorboards divided into diamonds of coloured gloss and clear matt varnish are attractive but can be slippery.

job. Fit a coarse abrasive to the sander and work diagonally across the boards to remove ingrained dirt and previous polish or varnish. Overlap the strips by about 75mm and switch off when you reach the skirting so that the sander doesn't scratch the boards as you turn. Then sweep the floor and fit a medium abrasive. Now sand up and down along the grain, overlapping in the same way, and remember to switch off when you reach the wall as before. Sweep the floor and repeat, using a fine abrasive. Next, using a small belt sander, work round the perimeter of the room to sand awkward areas, remembering to sand along the grain. Sand by hand, using a shavehook and abrasive paper plus a sanding block to reach right into the corners. Finally sweep or vacuum, then damp mop, allow to dry and thoroughly dust before varnishing.

## SEALING

Allow three to four coats of varnish on floorboards for maximum durability and make sure that the floor is completely clean and dusted before you begin. Dilute the first coat with up to 10 per cent white spirit and brush along the grain. Leave it to dry completely, then sand lightly and dust off thoroughly with a soft dusting brush before applying the next and subsequent coats. (Top wood shades or coloured varnish with clear varnish if you don't want to increase the depth of colour.) The sealed wooden floor needs a minimum of maintenance: simply sweep up the dust, mop and buff to a shine.

Right: panelled walls give distinction to this Oriental-style setting. Above the dado, apricot ragged over silver grey brings together the colours used separately elsewhere in the room, while the wainscot beneath is colour washed in grey to co-ordinate.

Above: many paint techniques mimic the qualities of natural materials like marble, tortoiseshell, wood grain and bamboo. Capturing the spirit is more important than slavish imitation, as this table treatment shows. You can protect such pieces with clear varnish, but it may cause discoloration.

Right: nothing is what it seems in this imposing hall. The hardwood handrail, white marble floor and black marble surround are all fakes, created by the clever use of paint. Golden yellow walls make a warm contrast to the cool 'stone' of the black and white marble and emphasize the feeling of richness and luxury.

Prettier than plain walls and more adaptable than wallpaper, decorative paint techniques are deservedly popular – and quite easy to achieve. In fact, it's often simpler to sponge or rag an uneven wall than to aim for a conventionally flawless finish because 'broken colour', as the effect is termed by professional decorators, successfully camouflages awkward irregularities. Though the method of applying paint with a sponge or cloth may seem crude, the end result is surprisingly soft and subtle. If you want to opt for a background effect that's more translucent and watery in colour, consider the technique of colour washing. Here a delicate top coat modifies the underlying base colour. Stencilling produces positive, clear-cut patterns which are ideal for forming friezes and borders or for highlighting a particular feature in a room.

None of these processes requires any special knowledge, materials or skill. For sponging, ragging and stencilling, simply use an oil-based mid-sheen paint like Satinwood straight from the tin, while emulsion thinned with water is all that's needed for colour washing walls. When you've mastered the basics, you may want to experiment with some of the more sophisticated processes like marbling, dragging and rag-rolling. To accomplish these, you'll need a transparent oil or 'scumble' glaze, which is available from specialist decorators' shops. Mixed with oil-based stainers and white spirit, this glaze forms a slow-drying surface which gives you time to create the desired effect.

There's a place for paint techniques in every home, whether you want to decorate the walls, paint the floor or rescue an undistinguished piece of furniture from obscurity. You can paint on plaster, metal or wood, co-ordinating these surfaces with your chosen colour scheme for the price of a pot of paint. Follow our step-by-step guides to the popular paint techniques, and use the room settings shown here for inspiration.

Stencils can be simple (below) or sophisticated (above). Stylized motifs in single blocks of colour are best for designs which involve repetition, like a frieze; reserve more ambitious designs like the bird and bowl of fruit as individual features. It's not essential to complete the work at one attempt, for the beauty of stencilling is that you can supplement existing designs with new as you please.

The subtle shading created by sponging suits modern as well as traditional settings. Pale silvery grey is used to create a cool contemporary atmosphere and impact is added by the scarlet furnishings. Sealed floorboards have been given a frieze in red and green which defines the shape of the room and emphasizes the colours used in the furnishings.

**Which Technique?**
● **Bambooing** copies the characteristics of bamboo on to rattan or turned wood.
● **Colour washing** has an uneven, translucent effect formed by a top coat of thin colour.
● **Dragging** has a 'strie' or self-striped effect created by drawing a brush through wet glaze.
● **Marbling** is done by painting marble-like 'veins' over a blended background.
● **Ragging** paint on with a soft cloth results in bold swirls.
● **Rag-rolling** is done with a bolster of rags rolled up and down a wet glaze.
● **Sponging** colour over a contrasting ground gives a mottled finish.
● **Stencils** are made by painting a pattern cut from acetate or card.
● **Stippling** has a pin-dot effect created by dabbing a brush on to wet glaze.

**Successful Sponging**
- Use a sea sponge, not a synthetic one.
- Sponge with either an oil or a water-based paint.
- Choose a base coat of Satinwood for wood and metal, vinyl silk or matt for walls.
- Sponge two colours over the base coat for subtlety.
- Start by sponging in related shades (peach and honey over apricot white, for example, or cream and primrose over yellow).
- Don't overload the sponge.
- Try the effect on paper before you start.
- Leave each coat to dry before applying the next.
- Hide radiators or cupboards by sponging to match the walls.

ponging is simplicity itself. All you need is a sea sponge, a tin of emulsion or an oil-based mid-sheen paint (such as Satinwood) and an hour or two. You can sponge on furniture or on walls, use one colour, or two or three, create a new scheme or refresh existing paint. The only rules to remember are 1) always use a sea sponge, not the cellulose type, and 2) choose the paint with care. You'll need a Satinwood or eggshell base coat, for example, on woodwork or furniture. Silk or matt emulsion is a satisfactory surface for walls and either a water or an oil-based paint for the sponging process; emulsion dries more quickly, so be careful it does not create a hard, patchy effect rather than cloudy softness.

Above left: ivory sponged with rose-beige creates a soft background in this traditional room. The sponged colour contributes warmth and co-ordination, and brings plain walls to life.

Above right: apricot and honey are sponged over cream to cast a warm glow in this country cottage bedroom. The fireplace and doors have been colour-rubbed with apricot to incorporate them into the scheme.

For the best results, pick a medium-sized sea sponge with a crisp texture which will produce an interesting pattern. Small sponges are laborious to use and fragment the effect, so avoid them unless you are sponging furniture or accessories. A trial run before you start allows you to experiment with different colour combinations and helps you estimate the amount of paint the sponge will soak up and the design it will produce. Don't overload the sponge or you'll get heavy patches, drips and runs. Take care to change the position of your hand from time to time to vary the effect. If the sponge starts to look crushed, slice it open and continue sponging with the cut edge.

Choose related colours for your first

1 Paint the walls with matt or silk emulsion in the usual way and allow to dry. Pour a little of the paint for sponging into a paint tray, dip your sponge into it and remove the excess on the grooved slope. Try the effect on a piece of paper until you are satisfied with the result. Take care not to overload the sponge or the finish will look blotchy and may run.

2 Begin sponging from the top of the wall down, dabbing the paint on with broad, random movements. Remember to vary the direction of your hand from time to time and turn the sponge so that the pattern does not become too regular. Take care to avoid a build-up of colour at corners and by door and window frames and skirtings or it may look patchy.

3 Continue working on the wall until the surface is covered. Here, only one colour has been sponged on to the surface. You can apply a second colour if you wish, when the first coat is dry. Start at the top of the wall as before and overlap the areas already sponged so that the two colours merge, but make sure that the background is not completely obliterated.

attempts and save bold colour contrasts until you are more experienced. Two shades of the same colour sponged over a pale or dark background look particularly attractive, but don't choose colours which are too close to each other or the end result may be indiscernible. Apply the first colour with a wide, open movement until you have covered the furniture or wall. A second, lighter shade applied when the first has dried adds subtlety and ensures that the background and the first coat merge. Sponging is a useful way to camouflage obtrusive features like pipes and radiators by colouring them to match the walls, but remember that you will need a Satinwood base for metal or wood which require a more durable paint than walls.

The humble rag has an important place in a variety of sophisticated paint techniques. Rags are used to rub colour into the grain of wood, to mottle backgrounds in advanced techniques like marbling and fossilizing, and to create pattern when rag rolling walls. The simplest way to use them, however, is in straightforward ragging, which is identical to sponging except that rags are used instead of a sponge. The result differs too, for ragging gives a bolder, more swirling design than the stippling produced by a sponge, and it's possible to alter the effect dramatically by changing the cloths you use. Mutton cloth or stockinette, with a crisp weave which softens during use, is a good, all-purpose cloth, but you can substitute cheesecloth, which makes a more sharply defined pattern, or use the folds of a close-woven cloth to create the impression. It's worth experimenting with a number of materials from chamois leather to cotton – anything

Below: fake 'panels' compensate for a lack of architectural features and correct or emphasize the proportions of a room. Here both panel and dado are ragged for interest and defined by a simple border.

Above: it takes only minutes to turn whipped cream into peach delight! This treatment was designed to blend with the colour of the blind and to echo the colour and pattern of the splashback.

**Successful Ragging**
● Remember that your choice of cloth can make a radical difference to the effect, so experiment with cheesecloth, muttoncloth, chamois leather and plain cotton
● Use an oil or water-based paint for ragging walls over an emulsion base
● Keep folding and crumpling the bunch of rags to produce a varied impression
● Discard rags as soon as they are clogged; use an airtight container for disposal if using oil-based paint

will work provided it's semi-permeable and lint-free – to choose which of the different effects you're happiest with.

Ragging 'on' in this way requires little expertise provided you remember to throw away the rags as soon as they become clogged and allow sufficient material to finish the room. (Take care when discarding rags if using oil-based paints. Don't smoke when decorating, or leave dustbin bags filled with paint-covered rags in the sun.) Remember to shake out and crumple the rags into a new shape regularly as you decorate to achieve a varied effect.

The paints recommended for ragging are the same as those used for sponging. Pattern is created with an oil- or water-based paint on a base of vinyl silk or matt emulsion on walls or Satinwood on furniture. When you have mastered ragging on, try your hand at ragging off and rag-rolling. Both of these techniques need a special glaze because it's important to keep the surface wet for as long as possible. They work by removing colour rather than applying it; so a mix of scumble glaze, white spirit and oil-based paint, is applied in strips and clean rags are used to create pattern, either crumpled into a ball for ragging off or twisted into a sausage shape for rag-rolling. Ragging on is the boldest of the three techniques, suited to bright modern colour schemes as well as to soft traditional ones. Ragging off is more subtle than ragging on because its effect relies on removing colour rather than applying it. Rag-rolling is a traditional technique that's especially appropriate in formal settings. It's the most complicated of the three and requires the most skill – in addition to working with a bolster of rags rolled up and down a wet glaze, it's also important to keep the pattern straight in order to achieve the desired effect. Stick to ragging on if you're a beginner and try ragging off once you've gained some expertise. When you're confident you can manipulate the glaze try rag-rolling – but until then leave it to the experts.

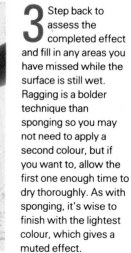

1 Paint the wall with a base coat of vinyl silk or matt emulsion in the colour of your choice; allow to dry. Pour a little oil-based mid-sheen paint or emulsion into a paint tray or dish. Now crumple up any lint-free rag – cotton, cheesecloth or stockinette – and dip it into the paint. Remove the excess on a piece of paper; this will also serve as a trial run.

2 When you are happy with the effect, start printing the wall. Work from top to bottom with a random movement, varying the way you hold your hand and stopping to fold the cloth in a different way from time to time. Renew the rag when the outline is no longer crisp; dispose of clogged rags in an airtight container to avoid fire risk if using oil-based paint.

3 Step back to assess the completed effect and fill in any areas you have missed while the surface is still wet. Ragging is a bolder technique than sponging so you may not need to apply a second colour, but if you want to, allow the first one enough time to dry thoroughly. As with sponging, it's wise to finish with the lightest colour, which gives a muted effect.

Below: add stencil patterns for instant Art Deco. These fans and flowers which replace cornice and picture rail sum up the style of this Thirties-inspired living room.

Flowers on the wall or fruit on the furniture can be yours for the asking with stencilling, the one paint technique which creates so much more than just abstract pattern. Stencils make a special contribution to home interiors; they are more flexible than wallpaper because you choose where to put the pattern. You can paint a border beneath a picture rail or around a fireplace, or create a single centrepiece. You can start with a simple geometric frieze and embellish it further whenever you like. As for the design, you can buy a stencil ready-made or you can adapt a motif from curtain fabric or upholstery to co-ordinate with furnishings.

Whatever you decide to use, the technique remains the same. For the best results, invest in a stubby pencil brush (available from artists' supplies shops) which keeps

Above: two separate borders in identical shades add definition at ceiling level and bring the blue-grey of upholstery and flooring into sharper focus. The simple geometric motifs are in keeping with the room's abstract shapes and uncluttered, simple design.

Left: shell designs find an appropriate home on this bath surround. (Acetate stencils are easier to use than card ones on curved surfaces.) The outside of the bath was coated with diluted PVA adhesive to prevent the tar-based paint from bleeding through, and then painted.

the colour inside the cut-out. (An ordinary artists' brush won't do because it allows paint to seep beneath the card.) Fix the stencil in place with spray photo-mount or double-sided tape, taking care to remove excess adhesive by sticking it on to fabric first so that it won't remove paint from the wall. When using a small stencil you can steady it with your hand, but don't use a product like Blu-Tak in place of tape as the stencil will stand proud and paint will leak underneath. Above all, make sure that the stencil is straight; it may be worth tracing faint guidelines on to the object you are painting, especially if you are working on a border, as it's only too easy to waver. Reversing the stencil creates an attractive symmetrical effect, but remember to wipe it clean every time you turn it round.

The ready-made stencils sold in stationers are ideal for beginners to use but it's not difficult to design your own. The most important point is to remember to leave sufficient ties to separate different areas; the white space is just as important to the pattern as the paint. Trace a motif and adapt it to form a stencil, and then enlarge it on a photocopier to the required size. The next step is to transfer the design on to oiled stencil card with carbon paper, or on to acetate by tracing it with a chinagraph pencil. A special craft knife is best for cutting the stencil though you can compromise with a trimming knife for simple designs. Leave a wide margin above and below the design to ensure its strength and remember to retain the original design in case the stencil breaks.

Although most paint techniques suitable for beginners are primarily designed for walls, stencilling is especially attractive when it's used to brighten up furniture or to create pattern on floors. Trompe l'oeil stencils provide a talking point, whether the subject is a vase of flowers above a (real) shelf or a patterned 'rug' on bare boards, but modest designs, using motifs or colours which combine with the furnishings, also have a valuable role to play.

**Successful Stencilling**
- Start with a simple single-colour geometric design.
- Use a special stubby stencil brush to keep the paint inside the cut-out areas.
- Dab rather than brush the paint into place.
- Fix the stencil to the surface with spray mount or double-sided tape to ensure that the paint will not bleed underneath.
- Always wipe the stencil clean before reversing it.
- Choose designs and colours which co-ordinate with furnishings so that stencils integrate with room schemes.
- Leave sufficient ties or bridges when adapting a design.
- Trace designs on to oiled card or acetate which can be cleaned with white spirit when making your own stencils.
- Make sure that the stencil is straight by drawing guidelines, especially when creating a frieze.
- Use stencils to decorate and brighten up furniture and floors as well as walls.

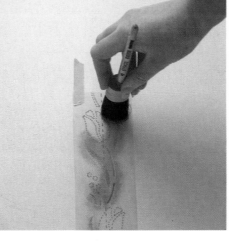

**1** Fix the stencil in place. Pour paint into a saucer, dip the stencil brush in and remove excess before dabbing into the cut-out areas.

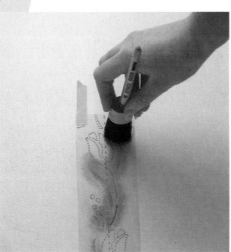

**3** Apply the second colour. Again dab the stencil brush into the cut out areas and make sure to remove excess paint before you start.

**2** Allow the paint to dry. If you are applying a second colour, you will need another stencil; carefully position it and then fix in place.

**4** When the stencil is complete, lift it carefully and move it on. Clean it thoroughly when you have finished.

**Successful Colour Washing**

● Use emulsion paints for speed and ease of use.
● Thin the top coat according to the manufacturer's instructions, given on the paint tin, in order to obtain the most manageable consistency and a translucent finish.
● Wait until each coat is dry before applying the next.
● Choose pale colours over white for a delicate effect; for a richer blend wash a deeper base coat in a related shade.
● Apply the wash with a wide wall brush used with a criss-cross, or random, movement.
● Leave some of the background exposed when applying the first coat of wash.
● Make sure that the second coat of wash covers the wall completely to achieve varying depths of colour.
● Use matt vinyl emulsion for a soft misty look, silk finish for translucence.
● Avoid a build-up of colour at corners and at skirting level.
● Beware of drips and runs which will spoil the effect.

Left: colour washes need not be confined to walls. These floorboards are coloured with thinned emulsion paint, by several coats of polyurethane varnish for protection. However, varnish will always cause some discoloration. The decorative stencil introduces pattern and picks up the colours of the rug it defines.

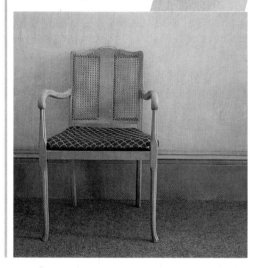

Colour washing creates the softest form of broken colour. Silver on white (far left) produces a gentle, hazy effect which matches the colour of the chair; the skirting is stained in a similar way to blend with the carpet. A pale aqua was chosen for both floor and walls in the bathroom (left). The treatment forms a subtle background for other paint treatments, such as the malachite on the mirror frame and the stencils which decorate both floor and blind.

The country cottage comes to town with this finish, a 'distressed' or faded effect with all the charm of colour which has softened with age. The material originally used for colour washing was distemper, the poor man's paint, but though you may still come across it in homes which are overdue for renovation, it's a product which is rarely used today. The chalkiness which gives distemper such an attractive appearance unfortunately makes it an impractical finish. It rubs away on your hands and on your clothes and no paint can adhere to it. Every scrap of distemper must be removed before it is covered with any other ma-

**1** When you have covered the wall with a base coat of full strength emusion paint, thin the emulsion chosen for the wash with water and try it for effect. Take the directions for diluting paint given on the tin as a general guide: too liquid a mixture will be runny, and is bound to drip; too little water added and the translucent effect will be lost.

**2** Now you are ready to apply the first coat of colour wash. Use a 50mm wall brush for this first coat and don't attempt to brush the paint on evenly – aim rather for a shaded effect. Move the brush in a random direction as you would when painting with a roller so that some areas have greater depth, but avoid runs and beware of creating a build-up of paint.

**3** Continue working up the first coat, but make sure you leave some areas of the background uncovered. When the first coat has dried, it will be ready for a second coat of wash. Dilute the paint as before and apply with a wide (100mm) wall brush, covering the entire wall this time. Again, brush the paint in a random, or criss-cross movement, exactly as shown.

terial, even another coat of distemper. The recommended treatment is to wash it away using a brush and plain water, then apply a stabilizing solution or plaster primer to seal the surface.

In place of distemper we now have emulsion paints containing vinyl, which can be washed rather than washed away. They may also be used for colour washing, one of the few decorative techniques where oil-based paints are not required. Simply paint the wall with the colour of your choice, and when it has dried apply two top coats of emulsion thinned with water to produce a translucent finish. (Thinned emulsion is also used on bare plaster as an initial 'fog' coat – this aptly sums up its misty effect.) Move the brush in a random direction (a process called cross-hatching) to vary the depth of colour and to avoid uniformity – colour washed walls should look patchy! Use matt vinyl emulsion for a velvety look, silk or satin vinyl for more watery colour. Finish with a coat of clear varnish if you want to increase the sheen, although it may cause yellowing and discoloration, and remember that it will have to be stripped before the walls are next repainted.

A more complex recipe for colour washing involves a top coat of glaze, oil-based paint and white spirit (the mix also used for advanced techniques such as dragging and rag-rolling). The effect produced here differs from that of the emulsion wash, but bear in mind that oil-based paints contain solvents which can make them unpleasant to use in large quantities. As emulsion paints are water-based the problem does not arise, and they are specifically designed for quick coverage. Remember to thin emulsion paint with water (not white spirit which is used for oil-based paints) and to experiment until you find a solution which produces the desired effect. And if you decide against the final result, it's the easiest thing in the world to obliterate it with a subsequent coat of full-strength emulsion paint.

Paint is more than just a pretty finish – it helps to protect the exposed surfaces from the ravages of time and weather – so never forget the outside of your house. Outside decoration needs few special skills and only becomes difficult if left for so long that preparation work becomes a major chore. The house illustrated below demonstrates the sorry results of a decade of neglect! You should reckon on redecorating the outside of your house around every four or five years; if you live in an industrial area or on the coast, however, the refurbishing job will have to be tackled more often in order to keep the effects of grime and the elements at bay.

Your efforts will repay you – remember that regular decoration shows the pride you take in your home, and it's also a sensible way of protecting your investment.

**Common Problems**
● Examine your house thoroughly. It's vital to eradicate damp and decay, otherwise paint will simply bubble and flake off within a few months. Where damage is very extensive you may need to call in the professionals.

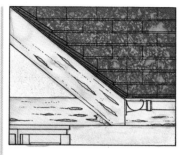

**1** Check fascias, bargeboards and decorative wood for rot, remove flaking paint and fill cracks.

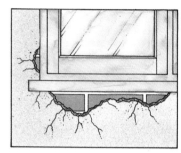

**2** Cut back defective rendering, clean and re-mortar. If damage is great, get professional help.

**3** Scrape flaking paint off metal downpipes, and brush; prime rust with anti-rust primer.

**4** Strip peeling paint on window sills and frames. Fill, sand, and treat knots before priming.

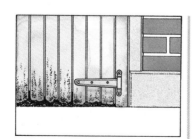

**5** Cut back wood beyond repair and renew it. Protect the bases of doors against damp.

**Primers**
● Universal Primers are for all surfaces. Dulux's covers 5-11 sq m per litre.
● Primer Undercoat does two jobs. Dulux's (suitable for wood inside and out) covers 11-13 sq m per litre.
● Dulux's Wood Primer covers 11-15 sq m a litre; for outside use, Dulux's Preservative Primer covers up to 20 sq m.
● Aluminium Wood Primer seals resinous wood. Dulux's covers about 16 sq m a litre.
● Metal Primers for exterior metal contain anti-rust agents. Dulux Q.D. Metal Primer covers 10 sq m a litre.
● Plaster Primer is for internal walls. Dulux's covers 9 sq m a litre.
● Stabilizing Primer seals surfaces that are still powdery after preparation. Dulux's covers 7 sq m per litre.

## PREPARATION

Check the house from top to bottom to estimate the extent of the work.

● Remove any decorations and tie back climbing plants.

● Check the roof and gutters and repair any leaks.

● Remove flaking paint and rust on metal downpipes and gutters with a wire brush, then prime areas with anti-rust primer (Dulux QD Metal Primer) or replace them entirely if the damage is irreversible. If existing paintwork is sound, sand it lightly to provide a key.

● Examine the fascias and bargeboards beneath the roof, window sills and frames for rot. Extensive decay must be cut away and replaced. Otherwise scrape damaged timber back to sound wood; repair with an exterior stopper like Dulux Weathershield Exterior Flexible Stopper. For paintwork in good order, clean, sand smooth and dust off before repainting. Sound, natural wood frames and smooth planed wood cladding need sanding lightly. Revarnish or treat with preservative stain like Dulux Wood-sheen. Strip defective varnish to bare wood, sand, and apply a first coat of exterior varnish thinned with white spirit. Use Dulux Timbercolour on rough-sawn wood such as sheds and fences.

● Replace cracked or broken window panes and renew putty. (Leave a week to harden before painting.) Fill gaps between wall and window frame with a flexible mastic.

● Clean out defective pointing and fill with a mixture of one part cement to four or five parts sharp sand.

● Repair defective patches in rendering with mortar.

● Brush outside walls thoroughly with a stiff brush from the top down before repainting.

● Treat mould with a solution of one part bleach to four parts water or Dulux Weathershield Fungacidal Solution. Leave for 48 hours, then remove with a stiff brush.

Don't fall down on the job! Make sure that ladders are secure, placed on a firm surface and, if possible, tied at the top. Use a proper extension ladder – don't try to get by with makeshift arrangements – and never use a ladder in a high wind. A paint kettle and S hook are essential so that you have one hand free for painting while you use the other to grip the ladder. Don't lean out, or back, too far, and never climb right to the top of a ladder or steps; the top of the ladder should always overlap the highest point.

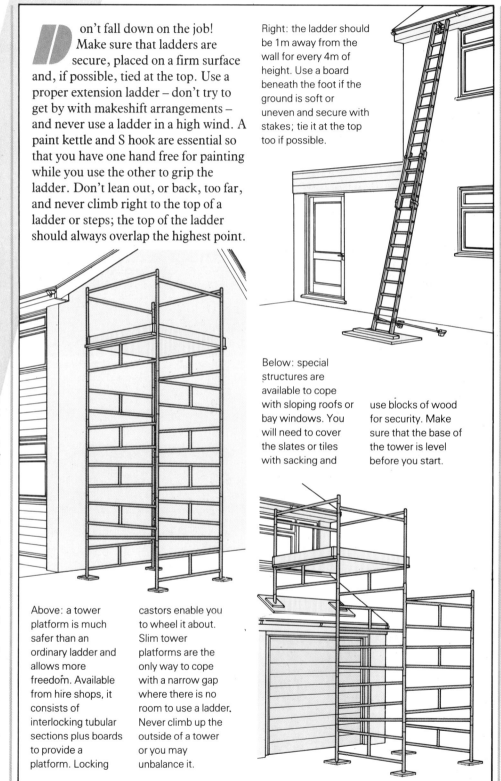

Right: the ladder should be 1m away from the wall for every 4m of height. Use a board beneath the foot if the ground is soft or uneven and secure with stakes; tie it at the top too if possible.

Below: special structures are available to cope with sloping roofs or bay windows. You will need to cover the slates or tiles with sacking and use blocks of wood for security. Make sure that the base of the tower is level before you start.

Above: a tower platform is much safer than an ordinary ladder and allows more freedom. Available from hire shops, it consists of interlocking tubular sections plus boards to provide a platform. Locking castors enable you to wheel it about. Slim tower platforms are the only way to cope with a narrow gap where there is no room to use a ladder. Never climb up the outside of a tower or you may unbalance it.

## MATERIALS

The products you choose for outside decorating must be durable and weather-resistant so check that the range which interests you is suitable for external use, and you'll need a water-based masonry paint for the walls.

If it's some years since you've painted the outside of your house you'll discover a big increase in the number of specialized paints and stains. The latest formulas provide better flexibility, plus resistance to fungus and moisture control. Gloss and masonry paints are now often colour co-ordinated to help you create the perfect exterior. Wooden sheds, summerhouses and fences also need protecting with a preservative like Dulux Timbercolour.

## EQUIPMENT

In addition to the tools used for interior decorating, you may need:
- a hot air gun for burning off paint.
- a stiff bristle brush for cleaning walls
- a brush for applying bleach or a fungacide
- a small trowel for mortar
- a long-handled crevice brush for painting behind pipes
- a paint shield
- a wide (100mm) paint brush for applying masonry paint in small areas
- a paint kettle and S hook
- a long pile roller for painting large areas of wall, plus an extension handle and paint tray. (Use a bucket plus a piece of wood to remove excess paint during ladder work.)

## ORDER OF PAINTING

Always start from the top and work down.
**1** Paint fascias, bargeboards and gutters.
**2** Paint the walls in sections, starting at the top right hand corner (unless you're left-handed), then treat the centre and the base.
**3** Paint the downpipes.
**4** Windows and doors are left until last.

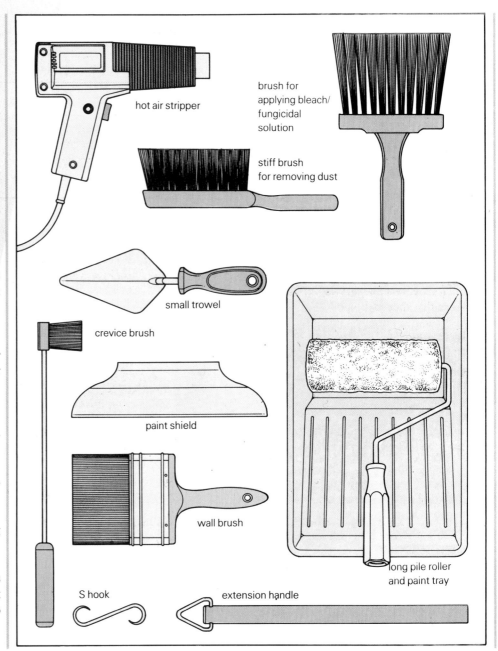

hot air stripper

brush for applying bleach/ fungicidal solution

stiff brush for removing dust

small trowel

crevice brush

paint shield

wall brush

long pile roller and paint tray

S hook

extension handle

# COVERAGE CHART

| Product | Coverage per litre | Recoatable |
| --- | --- | --- |
| Weathershield Exterior Undercoat (2 coats required) | 15 sq m | 16-24 hrs |
| Weathershield Exterior High Gloss | 17 sq m | 16-24 hrs |
| Weathershield Masonry Paint | 4-16 sq m | 1-4 hrs |
| Dulux Timbercolour | 5-10 sqm | |
| Dulux Woodsheen | up to 18 sq m | 16-24 hrs |

# PAINTING TECHNIQUES

**Woodwork** should be painted in the usual way. Using the Dulux Weathershield System, you will need one coat of gloss (plus primer on bare wood and two coats of undercoat) for protection. Paint the front door carefully – it's the first example of your work visitors see!

**Walls** are covered fastest by roller. Protect downpipes before you start by wrapping them in newspaper and cut in with a brush by bargeboards, doors and windows. Begin at the top and work up and down each section in bands about an arm's length across but *do not* lean out in an attempt to cover a greater area. Move the ladder along at regular intervals and overlap each strip slightly so that they merge.

### Painting Metal

First you'll need to provide a sound base for new paint. Remove any flaking paint with a scraper, then clean well with a wire brush to get rid of rust. Dust off, then prime bare areas with Dulux Q.D. Metal Primer.

Ensure that the surface is clean and dry. Using the Dulux Weathershield Exterior Gloss System, you will need to apply only one undercoat and one coat of gloss. Use a piece of board to protect the wall when painting pipes.

### Painting Exteriors

- Always read the can instructions carefully.
- Choose a fine, dry day for decorating.
- Follow the sun as you paint to ensure that surfaces are dry.
- Try not to paint in direct sunlight.
- Cover adjacent paths and plants with polythene to reduce the risk of splashing.
- Take care not to splash paint on brick; it will not come off.
- Disguise pipes by painting them to match the walls. Paint plastic pipes and guttering with conventional gloss, but don't paint plastic windows.

**1** Repoint the wall and fill big cracks with sand and cement mixture. Fill small cracks with exterior flexible stopper.

**2** Wipe off mould growth. Paint affected area with a bleach solution. Leave for 48 hours and then rinse.

**3** Clean the wall soundly with a stiff bristle brush to remove dust. Scrape off flaking paint and residual mould.

**4** Wrap downpipes in newspaper or polythene. Protect paths and plants with dust sheets in case of splashes.

**5** Use a wall brush for applying masonry paint in small areas. Remember to load the brush well for even coverage.

**6** Large areas are better tackled with a long-pile roller. Apply masonry paint with a random, criss-cross movement.

The publishers would like to thank the following companies for supplying merchandise:

All paints were supplied by Dulux/ICI plc.

All stencils were supplied by Carolyn Warrender Stencil Designs, suppliers of pre-cut stencil kits, specialist paints and brushes. Readers may obtain details of her mail-order service by writing to or phoning her at this address: Carolyn Warrender Stencil Designs, 1 Ellis Street, London SW1X 9AL, 01-730-0728.

**Hall** (pages 48/49): rug, The Conran Shop; hall table, dresser and chairs, Saville Pine; coat stand, The Pine Mine; blind fabric, Osborne & Little; selection of outdoor clothes, Gordon Lowe; dining table and bentwood chairs, Anvil Antiques.

**Dining Room** (page 52): parma table and bentwood chairs, Reject Shop; white china, accessories, glasses and cutlery, Coloroll; primrose paper border, Dulux; lamps, Christopher Wray; trolley and white curtain fabric, Habitat; seat cushion fabric, Decorator Collection/Laura Ashley.

**Kitchen** (pages 64/65): doors for kitchen units, W.H. Newsons & Sons Ltd.; chairs, Porky Arkwright; fabric for blind and tablecloth, Osborne & Little; light fitting, Mr. Light; picture and table in hallway, Sasha Waddell; ceramic floor tiles, Worlds End Tiles; stencils, Carolyn Warrender Stencil Designs.

**Modern Living/Dining Room** (pages 68/69): sofa, cushions, rug, dining table, chairs, lamps, china, cutlery and curtain fabric, The Conran Shop, 77 Fulham Road, London SW3; posters, The Poster Shop.

**Traditional Living Room** (pages 70/71): curtain fabric, cushions and sofa from The English Garden collection at Next Interior branches; wall lights, Jones, 194 Westbourne Grove, London W11.

**Bedroom/Bathroom** (pages 76/77): bedlinen and towelling designed by Primrose Bordier for Descamps; bed, bedside tables, trunk, chest of drawers, Saville Pine; stencils, Carolyn Warrender Stencil Designs; cushions and pictures from Five, Five Six Antiques, 556 King's Road, London SW6; basin, taps and towel rail, C.P. Hart; shutters, Plantation Shutters, 83 Antrobus Road, London W4.

**Baby's Room** (pages 78/79): bedroom units, Magnet & Southerns plc; cork tiles, Wicanders Ltd.; rug, Peter Jones; toys, Toys "R" Us (UK) Ltd.; bedlinen and accessories, Mothercare.

**Child's Room** (page 80): bunk beds, Texas Homecare DIY Stores; red/white metal storage trolley, Peter Jones; rug and director's chair, Habitat branches; accessories and stationery, Scribbler; bedlinen, Mothercare branches; sports clothes and equipment, Cobra Sports.

**Teenager's Room** (page 81): bedlinen, director's chair, rug, cushions, cupboard handles, anglepoise lamp, Habitat branches; posters, The Poster Shop.

Photographic Acknowledgments

Amdega Conservatories: 87br
Bo Appeltofft: 8r, 17l, 18b, 20br, 23br, 41l, 82b
Arcaid/Richard Bryant: 40br, /Tim Soar: 28br
Michael Boys: 28l, 55br, 89bl, 91tc, 103b, 110c
Christian Braud: 27
Camera Press: 6, 7, 9b, 16br, 37b, 38, 40bl, 41r, 45c, 45tr, 50-1, 61t, 66bl, 86bl, 87tr
Tommy Candler: 90–1b
Dragons of Walton Street: 45br
Futon Company: 110t
Goodwin Dorman Ltd: 14tl, cr, b
Lars Hallen: 16cr, 37t, 61t
Nelson Hargreaves: 8l, 9t, 9c, 11t, 11br, 22bl, 23tl, 50b, 51b, 97t
ICI Paints Division: 16L, 17R, 19R, 20-21T,
24BL, 26BR, 30, 32, 34, 39T, 39B, 40T, 44-5, 50T, 51T, 54-5, 62-3, 63B, 66-67T, 72TL, 72BL, 72-3, 73R, 74-5T, 75TR, 75B, 99, 101, 103T, 103C, 106, 109, 111B
Maison Francaise: 61b, 116tr
Maison de Marie Claire /Bouchet /Rozensztroch: 12–13, /Eriaud /Comte: 62l, /Girardeau /Hirsch Marie: 24cr, /Mouries /Sabarros: 26bl
Marston & Langinger: 86–7
Mitchell Beazley Ltd: 15t, c, b
Moygashel: 42t
National Magazine Company: 10t, 19tl, 31, 43r, 66–7, 112l
Orbis Books: 22tr, 24tl, 28, 54, 110r, 112–3, 116, 118cl, 118tr, 118br
P.W.A. Services: 23bl
Fritz von der Schulenberg: 46, 93
Sharps Bedroom Furniture: 74l
Smallbone & Company: 10b, 18t, 42–3, 44l
Jessica Strang: 20bl, 84t, 111t
Ron Sutherland: 97bl
Syndication International: 42b
Elizabeth Whiting & Associates /Karl-Dietrich Bühler: 89t, /Michael Dunne: 26tl /Clive Helm: 56l, /Ann Kelley: 88bc, br, 90tc, /Tom Leighton: 11bl, /Judith Patrick: 91b, /Spike Powell: 47, 84b, 116tl, /Tim Street-Porter: 60b, /Jerry Tubby: 12b, 13, 60t, 89br, 114r, /Carol Yuan: 91tl
World of Interiors /Francois Halard: 55tr, /Tom Leighton: 24–5, /James Mortimer 83tr
All other photography: Martin Chaffer and Simon de Courcey Wheeler
Jacket photography: Martin Chaffer

'COME HOME TO COLOUR'

*Large colour samples, decorating ideas and practical tips from Dulux*

**M**any of us play safe when decorating simply because it's difficult to assess how the tiny chip of paint on the colour card will look on a wall 5 metres long by 2.5 metres high! So to help consumers, Dulux have introduced a low-cost pack *Come Home to Colour*, which provides extra-large, edge-matched chips grouped in the popular colour themes of pink, peach, blue, brown, yellow, green and soft shades of white plus pictures of room settings to inspire you, as well as practical advice: in fact, all you need to create a successful colour scheme. In addition, there's advice on planning, lighting, using natural wood finishes such as Dulux varnish, and decorating the outside of your house. To complete the kit there are DIY tips and a guide to decorative paint treatments.

Many of you may be inspired by this book to try your hand at interior design, but if you still lack confidence with colour or have a difficult problem to solve, Dulux offers a panel of experts who will help create individual colour schemes for a small fee. Two examples, which show the detailed advice you can expect to receive, are displayed here.

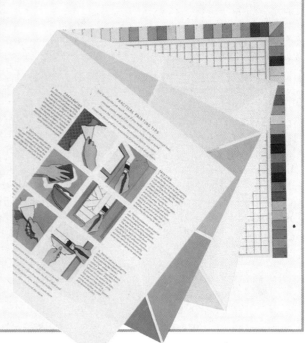

To obtain a similar personalized scheme, fill in the question-naire included in the pack, which requests information on relevant aspects of your lifestyle as well as your room. Bordering the grid on which you're asked to draw a simple plan of the room are colours which are used to indicate the shades of existing furnishings, so the colour consultants can be sure of producing a scheme which suits you, your home and your possessions. Send it with your cheque to the address given on the form and allow four weeks for completion – then it's over to you to translate the experts' ideas into reality.